FAITH, FINANCES, AND THE FUTURE:

The Notre Dame Study of U.S. Pastors

CATHOLIC EDUCATION STUDIES DIVISION

Alliance for Catholic Education Press
at the University of Notre Dame

FAITH, FINANCES, AND THE FUTURE:

The Notre Dame Study of U.S. Pastors

Ronald J. Nuzzi
James M. Frabutt
Anthony C. Holter

ALLIANCE FOR CATHOLIC EDUCATION PRESS
at the University of Notre Dame

Notre Dame, Indiana

To current and future
Catholic school children, including
Matthew, Jacob, Joshua, and Isabella Frabutt
Anna Elizabeth Holter

Alliance for Catholic Education Press
at the University of Notre Dame
158 IEI Building
Notre Dame IN 46556
http://www.nd.edu/~acepress

Text design, cover photograph by Julie Wernick Dallavis
Cover design by Mary Jo Adams Kocovski

ISBN 978-0-9788793-5-8

Library of Congress Cataloging-in-Publication Data

Nuzzi, Ronald James, 1958-
   Faith, finances, and the future : the Notre Dame study of U.S. pastors / Ronald J.
Nuzzi, James M. Frabutt, Anthony C. Holter.
      p. cm.
   Includes bibliographical references.
   Summary: "Examines demographic information, current and future school-related
needs, and attitudes and perceptions of U.S. pastors regarding their leadership of
Catholic schools"--Provided by publisher.
   ISBN 978-0-9788793-5-8 (pbk. : alk. paper)
   1. Catholic schools--United States. 2. Catholic Church--United States--Clergy--
Attitudes. 3. Educational leadership--United States. 4. Educational surveys--Unit-
ed States. I. Frabutt, James M., 1972- II. Holter, Anthony C., 1977- III. Title.

   LC501.N89 2008
   371.071'273--dc22
                        2008041114

This book was printed on acid-free paper.

Printed in the United States of America.

Contents

Acknowledgments

To J. Stephen O'Brien and John Convey,
whose pioneering research established the foundation for this study.

To Caroline Holter,
who assisted us in our efforts to contact pastors.

To the pastors themselves,
who gave willingly of their time and insights, and shared openly the needs and challenges facing Catholic schools.

To our friends and colleagues at the University of Notre Dame,
whose support and partnership were instrumental in this effort. We share a collective confidence that our commitment to research excellence will advance the field of Catholic education.

Executive Summary

While many challenges face Catholic schools today, it is clear that pastors are indispensible to addressing and overcoming these challenges. In fact, *The Code of Canon Law* (Caparros, Theriault, & Thorn, 1993) defines the centrality of the pastor in regard to the parish Catholic school. As highlighted by the Notre Dame Task Force on Catholic Education (2006), pastors' leadership and vision are vitally essential to the future of Catholic schools. Despite their importance as key stakeholders in Catholic education, few systematic attempts have been made to elicit their views on Catholic schools and there have been no such attempts in the last 10 years. Thus, given the nature of the Church, the importance of the parish in Catholic life, and the stipulations of Canon Law, there was a dramatic need to extend and refine existing research on priests' perception of Catholic schools.

The Notre Dame Study of U.S. Pastors directly addressed that need. Participants for this study were just over 1,000 U.S. pastors of Catholic parishes with schools that completed an electronic, Web-based survey. The study employed both quantitative and qualitative methods to obtain data regarding the questions of interest. The quantitative method components allowed for statistical analysis of survey data, including hypothesis testing, and were complemented by the qualitative components that provided rich, verbatim data from pastors. This mixed-method approach yielded an extensive data set that facilitated a robust analysis of a complex phenomenon: pastors' needs, perceptions, and attitudes regarding Catholic schools.

Major quantitative findings indicated that regardless of location of the parish school, pastors consistently identified Catholic identity and finances as the two most important needs facing their schools. Pastors identified the top five areas that their parish school was currently addressing: finances, marketing, long-range planning, enrollment, and Catholic identity. The data also revealed that as pastors' age, years of ordination, and Catholic school experience increase, so too does their agreement with the factors representing worth, value, access, and governance of Catholic schools. Findings demonstrated that pastors of parishes with schools who perceive the mission of their school to be supported by Catholic institutions of higher education demonstrate significant, positive increases in their evaluation of the worth, quality, access, and governance of Catholic schools compared to pastors who do not perceive such college or university support.

Qualitative findings indicated that pastors cited the most important needs facing their parish school as enrollment management, financial management, maintaining affordability,

> *Major quantitative findings indicated that regardless of location of the parish school, pastors consistently identified Catholic identity and finances as the two most important needs facing their schools.*

capital improvements, and Catholic identity. When asked to comment openly on Catholic schools and Catholic school leadership, pastors' responses centered on embracing Catholic identity and instilling the faith, financial management, valuing Catholic schools, leadership, and the need for Catholic school families to attend Mass.

Qualitative findings indicated that pastors cited the most important needs facing their parish school as enrollment management, financial management, maintaining affordability, capital improvements, and Catholic identity.

Recommendations flow broadly from the two major thematic areas voiced most by the participating pastors: finances and faith. Financial recommendations include more effective cost management in the realm of health care, increasing revenues through strategic development efforts, leveraging the power of pooled investments, aggressive pursuit of federal and state funds, and continued advocacy for school choice. Recommendations in the area of faith and Catholic identity include: conscious integration of the school community into the overall life of the parish, broader public parish leadership roles for school faculty, staff, administration, students, and parents, spiritual renewal of teachers and administrators, embracing education as a model for all ministry, and strategic engagement of the clergy in support of Catholic schools. Further research is needed to determine the best vehicles for addressing these concerns in a unified way, perhaps with the broader engagement of Catholic institutions of higher learning, the philanthropic community, and other Catholic leaders and stakeholders. The authors proffer that the deeper unifying challenge behind these issues is theological in nature and calls for serious reengagement with the core beliefs of Catholicism, renewed understanding of the central mysteries of the faith, and a fully realized evangelization and education of adult and young Catholics.

Introduction

There are many challenges facing Catholic education that are well chronicled in current research. Declining enrollment, financial shortfalls, lack of availability of highly qualified teachers and administrators, school closings, state and federal policy initiatives, and shifting governance structures (Gray & Gautier, 2006). A reasonable observer might ask, given these significant issues, why study pastors? The answer to the question involves the nature of the Church, the centrality of the parish in Catholic life, the understanding of the role of the pastor as delineated in *The Code of Canon Law* (Caparros et al., 1993), and the need to extend and refine existing research on priests' perception of Catholic schools.

This introduction contextualizes the Notre Dame Study of U.S. Pastors by describing the recent impetus behind this effort, reviewing Canon Law, as well as recounting past inquiries into this topic. A few systematic attempts to ascertain priests' perceptions about schools have already been conducted. Those, along with other pertinent investigations, are reviewed to provide an overview of the knowledge base as it currently stands.

Inquiry Sparked by the Notre Dame Task Force on Catholic Education

When the Notre Dame Task Force on Catholic Education released its 2006 final report, *Making God Known, Loved, and Served: The Future of Catholic Primary and Secondary Schools in the United States*, it proffered 12 action points for revitalizing Catholic schools that the University was poised to embrace. The Task Force itself convened in response to the bishops' statement, *Renewing Our Commitment to Catholic Elementary and Secondary Schools in the Third Millennium* (United States Conference of Catholic Bishops [USCCB], 2005). One of the action points described the notion of effective parish school leadership teams. The report noted that

> while supportive pastors are vital for parochial schools to thrive, the declining number of priests, among other factors, continues to increase the workload of pastors. Now more than ever we see the importance of collaborative leadership among pastors, principals, and school boards to ensure a vibrant parish school. (p. 12)

The report referenced a series of workshops (i.e., National Parish School Leadership Team Workshops) to foster joint, collaborative structures for pursuing best practices in leadership, marketing, strategic planning, and fostering Catholic identity. The desired end goal was "a replicable national model to galvanize more effective leadership that recognizes the pastor's role and enhances the administrative practices associated with Catholic schools" (p. 12).

Beyond Notre Dame's commitment to press forward on Catholic school leadership at the parish level, the report delineated five major recommendations to the broader Church community. One of them was directed specifically toward "the call for all pastors and priests to give vigorous support to Catholic schools in word and action" (p. 15). Noting that Catholic schools represent one of the most compelling ways for parents to instill the Catholic faith in their children, the report stated that "pastors have a special responsibility to proclaim this truth and do what they can to encourage and enable families to attend" (p. 15). The report asked, "how frequently and effectively do pastors use the pulpit to encourage and challenge parents" to embrace Catholic schools as a natural way to fulfill the promises of their children's baptism? (p. 15).

Notre Dame's Alliance for Catholic Education spearheaded an initial foray into examining parish school leadership through a series of focus groups held in summer 2007. These workshops convened leadership (i.e., pastors, principals, and school board presidents) from six Chicago parishes in June and several Holy Cross parishes in July. Qualitative data from those gatherings revealed wide divergence among pastors regarding the general importance of Catholic schools. Views spanned the continuum from highly supportive, "both from catechetical and practical perspectives—to questioning as to whether or not Catholic schools truly are effective at transmitting Catholic identity" (*Study on Parish-School Governance*, 2007, p. 2). Other discussions underscored the critical relationship between pastor and principal in "maintaining a similar understanding and regard for the mission of the school as a Catholic institution and its purpose as a ministry of the parish" (p. 2). The numerous anecdotal comments and richly textured personal reflections provided by pastors at these workshops illustrated the diversity of their thoughts and opinion on Catholic schools. Grounded in that qualitative data, the Notre Dame team clearly recognized the need to conduct a broad, nationally representative inquiry into this topic in order to understand the phenomenon more deeply. Thus, a major impetus behind the current study was the critical need to hear the voices of a key group of leadership stakeholders, pastors of parishes with elementary schools.

Importance of Pastors and Their Role in the Church

The Catholic Church has an overarching organizational structure that divides the entire landmass on Earth into regional church areas known as dioceses (Caruso, 2004a). No matter where one goes, it is impossible not to be in some diocese. Outsiders may consider such a worldview to be the result of hubris, but the deepest and original meaning of the term "catholic" is universal. In fact, "the basic unit of the church is the diocese" (Archbishop Pilarczyk as cited in Christopher, 1997, p. 7A). Dioceses are typically under the pastoral care and jurisdiction of a diocesan bishop, who is responsible for the overall well-being of all the people and institutions in his care. Moreover, all dioceses are similarly structured into smaller, even more regional units called parishes. One important way that a bishop cares for and leads his diocese is by ordaining, appointing, and supervising priests to serve and lead in these parishes. Pastors are these leaders.

In a fundamental way, pastors are the episcopally appointed regional leaders of the local Church. They are delegated by the bishop to exercise oversight and care for the spiritual and temporal welfare of everyone in the parish. Pastors are ultimately responsible to the diocesan bishop and serve at his pleasure. As such, their ministry, presence, leadership, and skills are vital and essential to parish life. Little can succeed without their blessing, while great things can happen with their support (Sweetser, 2007; Sweetser & Holden, 1992; Sweetser & McKinney, 1998; Zech & Miller, 2007).

For most Catholics, the parish provides the strongest connection to Catholic life (Brausch, 2003; Walch, 1996). The parish offers a liturgical life in keeping with the wider Church's calendar, serves as a nexus for sacramental celebrations including regular celebrations of the Eucharist, and is the gathering place for all of the faithful on the Lord's Day (John Paul II, 1998). Parishes also offer a variety of ministerial opportunities and community-building activities, as well as targeted programming, developmentally appropriate, to encourage the lifelong religious formation of all believers. In U.S. Catholic history, the most successful means of evangelizing youth and handing on the beliefs, traditions, and cultural mores of one generation to the next has been the Catholic school (Buetow, 1970, 1985, 1998; National Conference of Catholic Bishops, 1972).

Pastors are ultimately responsible to the diocesan bishop and serve at his pleasure. As such, their ministry, presence, leadership, and skills are vital and essential to parish life. Little can succeed without their blessing, while great things can happen with their support.

While fiscal crises and enrollment trends are indeed pressing issues worthy of study, this inquiry focuses on pastors because of their centrality in parish life, their leadership role in all pastoral and temporal affairs, and their ability to influence other leaders, including their bishops, on matters of Church policy and pastoral care. The important role of the pastor is articulated clearly in *The Code of Canon Law* (Caparros et al., 1993).

Canon Law on Pastors

In Book II, "The People of God," under Title III, The Internal Ordering of Particular Churches, *The Code of Canon Law* (Caparros et al., 1993) delineates at great length the various rights and responsibilities of a pastor. The pastor must see to it that the Word of God in its entirety is preached to those living in the parish. He must instruct the faithful on the truths of the faith. He is to be diligent in planning and executing Sunday worship, and especially dedicated to preparing and preaching a homily, which is mandated on Sundays and holy days of obligation. He is to foster social justice, care for the sick and dying, and make every effort to reach out to those who have stopped practicing their faith or who do not profess any faith (Canon 528, §1).

It is the pastor's responsibility to lead the parish in such a way that the Eucharist is the center of parish life, assuring that the faithful are regularly nourished through celebrating the sacraments. He is to see that parish liturgical life flows outward into families and individual households, so that a rhythm of prayer is established throughout the parish, and that this rhythm bears fruit in inspiring an active participation of the faithful in the sacred liturgy and in lives of Christian service (Canon 528, §2).

Pastors have a special obligation to come to know the faithful who live in the parish. They are obligated to visit families and share their cares and worries, and especially the griefs of the faithful. They are directed to show special solicitude for the poor, the afflicted, the lonely, and those who are exiled from their homeland (Canon 529, §1). Pastors are obligated by law to offer Mass for the people of the parish every Sunday (Canon 534).

All sacramental celebrations fall under the jurisdiction of the pastor, as does the record keeping for the same. The pastor has responsibility for all the temporal goods of the parish as well, represents the parish in public affairs, and is obligated to administer the parish in accord with the norms of law (Canon 532). Canon 533 ensures that the pastor will be available to the people of the parish, requiring that he reside in a parish house close to the church. Furthermore, he may be absent from the parish on vacation for at most one continuous or interrupted month, and he is to inform the diocesan bishop whenever he is to be away from the parish for more than a week (Canon 523, §2).

Because of the pastor's centrality in the life of the parish—his authority, liturgical leadership, administrative duties, pastoral responsibilities, educational oversight, relationships with his people, and even his physical proximity—no description of parish life would be complete without his participation.

In the area of Catholic education, *The Code of Canon Law* is terse, but direct and clear: "Pastors of souls have the duty to arrange all things so that all the faithful may enjoy a Catholic education" (Canon 794, §2). Catholic religious formation and education are among the most important activities of a parish and therefore of its pastor. In some sense, all activities, celebrations, liturgies, fundraising events, and social gatherings in a parish are educative in as much as they support the faithful in learning and experiencing life in Christ as part of a community. But educational efforts such as Catholic schools and religious education are more formal, structured approaches to the goal of the pastoral formation, evangelization, and salvation of the faithful.

Because of the pastor's centrality in the life of the parish—his authority, liturgical leadership, administrative duties, pastoral responsibilities, educational oversight, relationships with his people, and even his physical proximity—no description of parish life would be complete without his participation. It is simply not possible to understand, assess, change, or improve parish life without reference to the pastor.

The Parish School

The typical parish elementary school, positioned next to the parish church and carrying its name, is one of the great inventions of the Catholic Church and among its most successful evangelization efforts (Greeley, McCready, & McCourt, 1976). While the current climate in Catholic education has fostered some new and emerging governance structures, such as interparochial schools and regional schools, consortium models and independent Catholic schools, the school as a ministry of a parish remains a compelling and successful model.

It is important to note that in this traditional model of one parish school, the school itself remains a ministry of the parish, subject to the authority of the pastor. In *The Code of Canon Law* (Caparros et al., 1993), this involves the concept of a public juridic person.

According to the *Code*, a public juridic person is an entity capable of bearing rights and of being subject to duties just as if it were a natural person (Mallet, 1985). It is reasonably equivalent to the concept of a corporation in U.S. law. A public juridic person is a legal entity, able to do business, subject to other laws, and is separate from all physical or natural persons. It is a legal entity in its own right. A juridic person has duties and responsibilities, can own property, and be held liable for its actions.

Juridic personality is itself conferred by *The Code of Canon Law* and many organizations in the Church have this status. Dioceses, parishes, and seminaries are common examples of juridic persons. While it is common for a diocesan sponsored Catholic high school to have this status, parish schools by definition do not. Catholic schools that are a part of parishes are not technically independent or autonomous entities. In such cases, the school is a part of the juridic person of the parish and is not a separate entity or corporation. Although it may often appear differently because of the manner in which administrators operate, funds are distributed, and resources are used, there is no canonical distinction between a parish and its school. They are technically one and the same.

This important distinction also serves to highlight the role of pastor in the parish school, for although the pastor delegates his authority to a school principal for the administration of the school, the pastor remains the one ultimately responsible for all parish operations and ministries. Thus, the parish school, as a ministry of the parish in whose juridic personhood it resides, is always under the direction of its proper pastor.

Commentary and Scholarship on the Pastor-School Relationship

Having reviewed the role of the pastor as delineated in the *The Code of Canon Law* (Caparros et al., 1993), the final section of this introduction describes the thread of research and scholarship that has investigated the pastor-school relationship.

Early References to the Pastor-School Relationship

Some of the first references to the pastor-school relationship in academic journals seem almost quaint in retrospect. They are certainly based more on anecdote and personal experience rather than systematic attempts to examine the issue. Two examples follow. First, at an address given at the 1935 meeting of the National Catholic Educational Association (NCEA), Father Thomas B. O'Brien discussed the new wave that had swept the country: the superintendent. He spoke of the initial threat that many pastors felt at the thought of an outside examiner or supervisor insinuating themselves into the operating of a parish school:

And the pastor had suspected that the school superintendent had concealed on his person a microscope and a big stick or the torturing end of a crozier. Yes, the pastor resented any supervision of his school. It was the apple of his eye, the pride of his life….His own personality, dominant and religious, had planted germs of virtue that had crystallized into a beautiful manhood and womanhood. (p. 417)

Clearly this was a pastor that loved his school and the ministry that went on within it. Anything that could possibly undermine that relationship was suspect. O'Brien did go on to extol the virtues of the superintendent role, noting its effectual impact on matters of leadership, pedagogy, diplomacy in personnel matters, and capital improvements.

Second, in an article entitled, "The Priest Visits His School," McMahon (1947) stressed that most fundamentally, the "priest is *the* teacher of religion in the parish" (p. 451, italics in original). His article presents a brief guideline for the pastor to play that all-important role for the children in the parish school. He notes that during the priest's weekly visit to the school, he should encourage children's probing questions about Christian Doctrine, teach via the use of parables, and reserve 10 minutes for "leading a meditation on one of the mysteries of the Rosary" (p. 454). The priest might also encourage the children to identify a "friend for life among the saints" as well as provide about two minutes of silent reflection time in class (p. 456). Lastly, McMahon stressed the importance of the priest's example at Mass as a way to teach prayerfulness. Since "children X-ray their teachers, and that includes their priests" (p. 455), the Mass itself is a teaching opportunity for the priest and a learning opportunity for the children.

Doctoral Dissertations Exploring the Pastor-School Relationship

Sullivan (1982) appears to be the first researcher to employ a survey methodology to surface the attitudes and perceptions of priests toward Catholic schools. Sullivan wrote that "it is no exaggeration to say that the pastors in the Archdiocese of Boston will be one of the most influential factors for or against the design for new schools in the Church of the 80's" (pp. 108-109). He noted that their perceptions would be "a critical determinant in the planning of the educational programs in the Archdiocese of Boston" (p. 109). Utilizing a jury of 14 experts, he developed, pilot tested, and refined the original questionnaire that has been used in several subsequent investigations. The survey consisted of background information, and 42 statements that priests rated either *agree, undecided,* or *disagree*. A random sample of 215 out of 300 priests from the Archdiocese of Boston completed the survey. Sullivan reported his findings according to the four areas in which priests' perceptions were assessed: the value, effectiveness, financial viability, and future structure of Catholic schools. Schipper (1982), building on Sullivan's dissertation, replicated the study with diocesan priests of the Archdiocese of San Francisco. A third dissertation, completed by Tacheny (1987), extended much of the same research questions and methodology to diocesan priests of the Winona and New Ulm dioceses of Minnesota.

A National Investigation of the Parish-School Relationship

J. Stephen O'Brien completed a dissertation in 1986 that was subsequently developed into the book, *Mixed Messages: What Bishops and Priests Say about Catholic Schools* (1987). That investigation was noteworthy because it was the most comprehensive and definitive inquiry into the perceptions of clergy toward Catholic schools. O'Brien's text begins by describing the historical context that gave rise to Catholic schools in the US. He traces several historical milestones—even preceding the birth of the nation—such as early schools emerging out of Spanish missionary activities to convert Native Americans. O'Brien recounts the outgrowth of the first Catholic schools, the growing dissatisfaction with the public schools, leading to the Third Plenary Council's exhortation in 1884 to found, finance, and support parish schools: "We must multiply them, till every Catholic child in the land shall have within its reach the means of education" (Guilday, 1932, as cited in J. S. O'Brien, 1987, p. 17). O'Brien describes the influx of southern European immigrants and the stressors that such rapid expansion placed on schools, both public and Catholic. He outlines the controversies among bishops regarding the necessity and value of two separate systems, culminating in the rapid growth of Catholic schools. He describes the coming of age of Catholic schools, and a growing stability in the American Catholic Church leading up to Vatican II. The closing section in O'Brien's historical sketch cites the dropping enrollment numbers that followed Vatican II and provides some rationale for their decline. One thing is certain, however, which lays the foundation for his survey: "Because of the wide-ranging authority given to them by the Code of Canon Law, pastors are very important to schools" (p. 46).

"Because of the wide-ranging authority given to them by the Code of Canon Law, pastors are very important to schools" (J. S. O'Brien, 1987, p. 46).

Based on that contextualizing information, J. S. O'Brien (1986, 1987), building on the earlier diocesan surveys (Schipper, 1982; Sullivan, 1982; Tacheny, 1987), directed a large scale, nationwide study to examine the perceptions of U.S. bishops, pastors, and future pastors regarding four domains: the (a) value; (b) effectiveness; (c) funding practices; and (d) future of Catholic schools. As Executive Director of the Department of Chief Administrators at the National Catholic Educational Association, O'Brien mailed an anonymous, confidential survey, via written questionnaire, to 273 bishops (219 responded; 80% response rate) and 660 priests (346 responded; 52%). With a cover letter from Archbishop Roach, president of the NCEA board of directors, the questionnaires were sent to the entire population of bishops and a random selection of pastors derived from the 1985 version of *The Official Catholic Directory*. Both surveys were comprised of two parts (53 items total). Part I contained 11 background/demographic items and Part II contained 42 items on a 4-point scale ranging from *strongly agree* to *strongly disagree*.

J. S. O'Brien's (1987) book devotes four chapters to unpacking the descriptive survey, one each for value, effectiveness, funding, and future structures. A major lens that O'Brien used to present his findings was to compare and contrast the responses of bishops and priests. For example, referring to an item that asked whether Catholic education afforded the fullest opportunity to realize the threefold purpose of Christian education (i.e., doctrine, community, and service), O'Brien reported that "the bishops overwhelmingly agreed that it did (99%). The priests were not so certain; only 76 percent of them agreed" (p. 62). In fact, an entire chapter, entitled "Unity and Diversity," is devoted to exploring the areas of highest and lowest agreement between bishops and priests. He concluded with seven suggestions for possible action: (a) need for a national study on the regionalization and centralization of Catholic elementary schools; (b) derive alternative financial plans for schools; (c) encourage bishops to seek federal aid; (d) conduct in-depth study of religious education programs outside of schools; (e) promote consultative educational bodies to strengthen schools' local governance; (f) provide curriculum materials on the value and effectiveness of Catholic schools to seminarians; and (g) encourage priests' personnel boards to appoint priests that value schools to parishes with schools.

Scholarship since *Mixed Messages*

Almost 10 years after the publication of *Mixed Messages*, Convey (1999) conducted a survey to update and expand the knowledge base on clerical and episcopal perceptions of Catholic schools. This timing was opportune and fortuitous; Convey noted that his study, in contrast to J. S. O'Brien's (1986, 1987), was conducted in a "context of increasing optimism concerning Catholic schools and their future" (1999, p. 249). Drawing on the item pool used in the earlier dissertations and *Mixed Messages*, the questionnaires consisted of demographic items and a common set of 64 sentiment items across four categories: worth, quality, access, and governance (see Table 1). Questionnaires were mailed to all bishops and a random sample of priests in each of three categories: pastors of parishes with schools, pastors of parishes without schools, and other clergy. Completed questionnaires were received via mail from 184 bishops and 1,026 priests representing 165 dioceses.

Table 1
Factors Assessed Via Convey's Questionnaire and Their Definition

Factor	Definition
Worth	Measures the need for Catholic schools and their importance
Quality	Measures the perceived effectiveness of Catholic schools
Access	Measures financial and other support needed to ensure access of families to Catholic schools
Governance	Measures support for parental participation in governance

Convey's (1999) analysis revealed several major findings among the priest sample. First, pastors from parishes with schools—compared with cooperating pastors, non-school pastors, associate pastors, other clergy, and retired priests—had the highest agreement with the worth, quality, and access factors. Second, Convey found significant correlations between time ordained and access, worth, and governance. Specifically, "priests ordained fewer than 21 years and those ordained more than 30 years have higher levels of agreement to both Access and Worth than do priests ordained between 21 and 30 years" (p. 256). A positive linear relationship was detected between years ordained and quality. Third, location of ministry was related to the access factor, such that "the more removed in terms of distance the ministry of a priest is from the inner city, the less supportive he is of issues pertaining to supporting Catholic schools financially, including sharing of resources to help non-parishioners attend Catholic schools" (p. 260). Fourth, priests who had themselves attended Catholic schools did not differ from those who did not on their assessment of the governance, quality, and access factors. While some differences emerged for worth, they were only operative among associate pastors and priests in other ministries.

A recent small scale investigation provided additional insight into the dynamics of clergy's perception of Catholic schools. Caruso (2004b) conducted a survey of seminarians, "Future Shepherds and Catholic Elementary Schools," to explore their perceptions regarding parish elementary schools and the possibility of their assignment to a parish elementary school. Caruso addressed his basic research question—"What are the perceptions of seminarians toward parish elementary schools?"—through a survey of 67 seminarians at St. John's Seminary in Camarillo, California (p. 68). The 32-item survey consisted of three sections: demographic information, Likert-scale endorsement of statements regarding Catholic schools and priests' role in those schools, and short answer questions eliciting challenges facing Catholic schools as well as their strengths. While the sample itself was ethnically diverse, it was geographically limited to the American West (although a few international seminarians were in the sample).

Results indicated that 76% of the sample *agreed* or *strongly agreed* with the statement: "As an associate pastor I hope to be assigned to a parish with a school" (p. 71). Sixty-seven percent endorsed a desire to seek a parish assignment as pastor. Seminarians were ambivalent, however, about the Catholic identity and culture of the schools. Caruso (2004b) observed low levels of endorsement of items that tapped other professionals' leadership in the school context versus high levels of endorsement of items that referred to clerical leadership. Caruso reasoned that "seminarians have a clear vision of their own pertinent school leadership abilities, skills, and knowledge. At the same time, it appears that the seminarians question the abilities, skills, and knowledge of other professionals working in the schools" (p. 72).

Purpose of the Current Study

The first in nearly 10 years, the Notre Dame Study of U.S. Pastors is a systematic analysis of pastors' needs and perceptions regarding Catholic schools and Catholic education. The study affirms the uniquely important leadership role of pastors in the parish and in the Catholic school. Its point of departure is a firm belief that the pastor is so important that no effort to serve Catholic schools can succeed without them. Engaging pastors in a national dialogue on Catholic education will lead to a clear and nuanced understanding of their needs, challenges, and leadership insights so that such information can be brought to bear on sustaining and strengthening Catholic schools.

The current study builds on and extends the lineage of national survey samples and replicates portions of J. S. O'Brien's (1986, 1987) and Convey's (1999) analyses. In addition, it collected open-ended, narrative responses to gather the verbatim comments of priests and thereby capture their sentiments in their own words. A new set of ground-breaking questions included a needs assessment to understand the valence of various focus areas for parish schools (e.g., marketing, technology, governance, faculty recruitment, etc.).

Engaging pastors in a national dialogue on Catholic education will lead to a clear and nuanced understanding of their needs, challenges, and leadership insights so that such information can be brought to bear on sustaining and strengthening Catholic schools.

Method

The Notre Dame Study of U.S. Pastors employed both quantitative and qualitative methods to obtain data regarding the questions of interest. The quantitative method components allowed for statistical analysis of survey data, including hypothesis testing, and were complemented by the qualitative components that provided rich, verbatim data from participant responses. This complementary, mixed-method approach yielded an extensive data set that facilitated a robust analysis of a complex phenomenon: pastors' needs, perceptions, and attitudes regarding Catholic schools (Green & Caracelli, 1997). Details regarding specific features of each method are provided below.

Participants

Participants for this study were U.S. pastors of Catholic parishes with schools (n = 1,047). It is important to note that all pastors did not answer all questions due to the voluntary response structure of the survey instrument. As such, differential sample sizes are reported in the Quantitative Findings section. Pastors were selected from a convenience sample of approximately 2,000 pastors with e-mail addresses who were contacted directly and invited to participate in the survey. Additionally, approximately 120 individuals (e.g., vicar for clergy, superintendent, central office personnel) were contacted and asked to forward the survey invitation to pastors in their diocese. The sample population represents approximately 17% of all U.S. pastors of parishes with schools, and is characteristic of the national demographics of pastors and geographic location of Catholic schools (McDonald & Schultz, 2008).

Survey Instrument

The Notre Dame Study of U.S. Pastors employed an electronic survey instrument that consisted of both original survey items and items adapted from the pioneering work of J. S. O'Brien (1986, 1987) and Convey (1999; see Appendix A). The survey instrument included 33 total items organized into three main categories: demographic information (e.g., age, years ordained, Catholic school attendance), needs assessment for the school (e.g., identify top five needs the parish school is currently addressing), and pastor's perceptions of and attitudes toward Catholic schools (e.g., the need for Catholic schools is at least as great today as in the past).

In addition to the forced-response items, the survey instrument prompted open-ended, narrative responses to gather the verbatim comments of priests and thereby capture their sentiments in their own words. These open-ended questions were first employed after the second category of survey items, the ground-breaking needs assessment questions designed to understand the valence of various focus areas for parish schools (e.g., marketing, technology, governance, faculty recruitment, etc.). Pastors were asked to respond to the following prompt: "In your own words, what are the most important needs facing your parish school in the next two to five years?" Additionally, an open-ended item was included at the end of the survey prompting pastors to "provide any additional comments regarding thoughts and opinions on Catholic schools or Catholic school leadership."

The third category of survey items assessed pastors' perceptions and attitudes of Catholic schools within four general categories: worth, quality, access, and governance. Pastors responded to these 23 questions using a 5-point Likert scale ranging from *strongly agree* (5) to *strongly disagree* (1). A factor analysis was conducted to determine if the a priori categories (Convey, 1999; J. S. O'Brien, 1986) were indeed statistically related. The data yielded a range of factor loadings from 0.62 to 0.83 for each category and accounted for 62% of the total variance. Furthermore, internal consistency reliability, as measured by Chronbach's alpha, was high for worth (α = .91), quality (α = .88), access (α = .85), and governance (α = .72). The high factor loading, percent of variance explained, and internal consistency reliability confirm that these a priori categories are clustered and do effectively function as subscales.

Design and Procedure

The Notre Dame Study of U. S. Pastors utilized a cross-sectional survey design, and was launched in January 2008. The study was implemented through a series of five phases to increase response rate and maximize the validity of the results (Dillman, 2007; Mangione, 1998; Schonlau, Fricker, & Elliot, 2002). A notice letter and e-mail (Phase 1) announcing the study were sent to over 100 diocesan contacts and nearly 2,000 pastors. Next, a personalized e-mail (Phase 2) with a link to the electronic survey was sent to pastors inviting them to participate in the study. The final three phases (Phase 3-5) involved follow-up and reminder e-mails encouraging pastors who had not yet completed the survey to do so. The implementation of the survey procedure spanned 2 months and was completed in March 2008.

Quantitative Data Analysis

The analytic software SPSS version 16.0 was used to conduct the quantitative analysis of the data. The raw data were coded and cleaned for any anomalous or inaccurate entries. Fifty participants were removed from analysis during this process due to significantly incomplete response sets. Next, descriptive statistics were calculated for each of the main categories of the survey instrument (demographic, school needs, and perceptions and attitudes). Descriptive statistics were used to identify general themes in the data. Finally, a partial replication of previous analyses (Convey, 1999) and additional inferential analyses were conducted using MANOVA, ANOVA, and correlation procedures to test the primary questions of interest. Further details on these procedures and analytic outcomes are included in the quantitative findings section.

Qualitative Data Analysis

For two open-ended survey items, verbatim responses from pastors were entered into NVivo 8 qualitative data analysis software. The software is a useful tool to support the overall goal of qualitative data analysis, which is to sift, sort, and organize masses of data—in this case, hundreds of written comments.

A systematic, multi-stage analysis process was utilized. Cleaned and formatted data for both items were read multiple times—what some authors describe as previewing the data—to gain familiarity with the scope and depth of the entire data set (Unrau & Coleman, 1997). As outlined below, the analysis approach varied slightly depending on whether the question assessed needs versus general pastor comments.

Qualitative Coding of Needs. The survey presented several response options in the two closed-ended questions (Questions 21 and 22) that preceded the open-ended item inviting pastor commentary on needs: "In your own words, what are the most important needs facing your parish school in the next two to five years?" (Question 23). Therefore, the response set for Questions 21 and 22 established, in effect, 16 a priori coding categories for Question 23. Text segments—individual meaning units—from the pastors' responses were selected one at a time and categorized into codes. Codes are essentially labels or tags assigned to descriptive information (Miles & Huberman, 1994). It soon became evident that many comments and emerging themes could not be categorized into one of the 16 established categories (i.e., codes). Thus, clusters of responses began to coalesce into new codes, adding to the list of initial themes. Ten distinct new codes were derived overall. It should be noted that in some cases, a text segment was double-coded when the content of the statement reflected two linked thematic areas.

Qualitative Coding of General Comments. The final item on the survey (Question 33) provided the open-ended prompt to pastors: "Please provide any additional comments regarding thoughts and opinions on Catholic schools and Catholic school leadership." Since no a priori coding scheme was established for this item and respondents had not been primed by an immediately preceding response set, a purely open coding approach was utilized. Via this open coding process, categories and meaning units emerged directly from the data. As categories began to form, each new text segment was evaluated using a constant comparative method, which essentially asks whether the data segment fits an existing category or begins to define a new one. Categories were created until thematic saturation was achieved. For this final open-ended item, 20 thematic areas were defined; more detail is provided in the second sub-section of the qualitative findings.

Quantitative Findings

Descriptive Statistics

In addition to the demographic data regarding the pastor participants, descriptive statistics were used to identify general themes and patterns in the final two sections of the survey instrument: needs assessment and pastors' perceptions and attitudes. The following is a general overview of the descriptive statistics.

Participant Pastor Characteristics

The average age of pastors participating in the study was 55.93 (SD = 9.77). Table 2 illustrates the distribution of pastors according to age groupings. The largest percentage of pastors (n = 390, approximately 37% of the total) was within the 56-65 age category. Additionally, the average number of years ordained was 26.88 (SD = 11.67). Table 3 shows the distribution of pastors according to years ordained. Congruent with the age demographics, most pastors (n = 321, approximately 31% of the total) had been ordained 31-40 years. Over 90% were diocesan priests, while approximately 10% were ordained priests in a religious congregation. Additionally, 35% of participants (n = 366) attended seminary at one of the top 10 seminaries with the highest enrollment in 2007-2008 (Gautier, 2008).

Table 2

Distribution of Respondents by Age Category (Years; n = 1,042)

Age Category	n Respondents	Percent Total
35 and under	22	2.11
36 – 45	150	14.40
46 – 55	300	28.79
56 – 65	390	37.43
65 and over	180	17.27

Participants were surveyed from each regional grouping as established by the NCEA (McDonald & Schultz, 2008). Table 4 shows the number and percent total of participants from each geographic region. The Great Lakes region—consisting of Illinois, Indiana, Michigan, Ohio, and Wisconsin—produced the largest number of participants (n = 308, approximately 29% of the total). It is important to note that the regional percentages of participating pastors roughly match the actual regional

Table 3

Distribution of Respondents by Ordination Category (Years; n = *1,040)*

Ordination Category	n Respondents	Percent Total
10 or less	117	11.25
11 – 20	229	22.02
21 – 30	241	23.17
31 – 40	321	30.87
41 or more	132	12.69

Table 4

*Distribution of Respondents by Region (*n = *1,044)*

Region	n Respondents	Percent Total	Actual Percent of Catholic Schools
New England	46	4.41	6.40
Mideast	253	24.23	25.00
Great Lakes	308	29.50	24.50
Plains	129	12.36	11.90
Southeast	154	14.75	12.80
West/Far West	154	14.75	19.40

distribution percentages of Catholic elementary schools (McDonald & Schultz, 2008). Additionally, the location of the Catholic elementary schools in inner-city, urban, suburban, and small town/ rural areas was recorded according to the guidelines set forth by the NCEA. Table 5 indicates the distribution of schools in these categories. Again, it is important to note that, although not identical to the national trends, the sample population schools closely match the national distribution of schools by location (McDonald & Schultz, 2008). Most of these schools serve a predominantly Caucasian student population (see Figure 1) and are structured in the PreK-8 model (see Figure 2).

Table 5

*Distribution of Respondents by Parish Location (*n = *1,034)*

Location	n Respondents	Percent Total	Actual Percent of Catholic Schools
Inner City	120	11.61	12.30
Urban	299	28.92	29.40
Suburban	300	29.01	36.20
Small Town/Rural	315	30.46	22.00

Figure 1. Primary race/ethnicity of the study sample (*n* = 1,021)

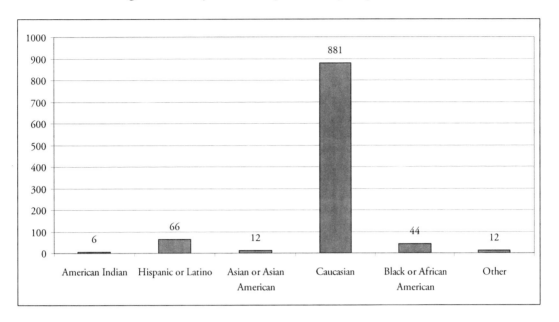

Figure 2. School structure (*n* = 911)

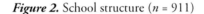

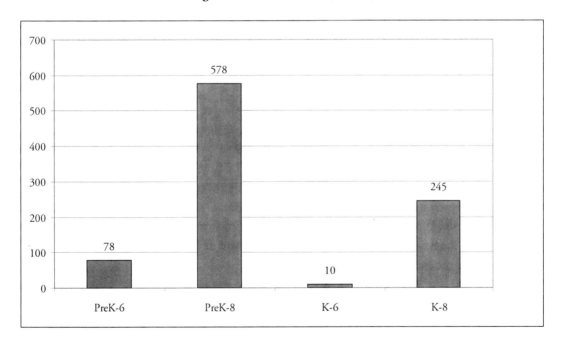

Pastors generally reported high attendance in Catholic schools for their own education as reported in Table 6. Seventy-four percent (*n* = 759) attended Catholic elementary school for at least 5 years. That percentage increases to over 80% when pastors with between 1 and 4 years of Catholic elementary school attendance are included. Pastors also reported high attendance at Catholic high schools (*n* =

Table 6
Distribution of Respondents by Catholic School Attendance (Years)

Catholic School Attendance		*n* Respondents	Percent Total
Elementary School (*n* = 1,020)	Did not attend	196	19.21
	1-2	28	2.75
	3-4	37	3.63
	5-8	759	74.41
High School (*n* = 1,012)	Did not attend	293	28.95
	1-2	26	2.57
	3-4	693	68.48
College or University (*n* = 1,013)	Did not attend	590	58.24
	1-2	100	9.87
	3-4	262	25.86
	5 or more	61	6.03

693, approximately 68% of the total). Relatively fewer pastors reported attending a Catholic college or university for any period of time (*n* = 324, approximately 42% of the total).

Survey data also indicated relatively high participation in and experience with professional positions in Catholic education. Over half of pastors (57%) had been teachers in a Catholic school, 22% had been an administrator, and 36% had been a chaplain at a school. Additionally, 32% of pastors had experience working in the diocesan office and nearly 4% had been superintendent of Catholic schools.

Needs Assessment

Using a 5-point Likert scale ranging from *extremely important* (5) to *not at all important* (1), pastors were asked to rate the importance of each area of need as it pertains to their school. Regardless of location of the parish school, pastors consistently identified Catholic identity (*M* = 4.63, *SD* = 0.75) and finances (*M* = 4.45, *SD* = 0.72) as the two most important needs facing their schools (see Figure 3). Similar results were obtained when pastors were asked to identify the top five areas that their parish school was currently addressing. The top five areas pastors indicated were: finances (*n* = 623), marketing (*n* = 579), long-range planning (*n* = 538), enrollment (*n* = 530), and Catholic identity (*n* = 528; see Figure 4).

Support

When asked for the most reliable source of information for decision making, pastors overwhelmingly indicated that the principal (*n* = 507) was the most reliable source. The next closest source was the school board (*n* = 138; see Figure 5). Using a 4-point Likert scale from *highest support* (4) to *no support* (1), Pastors again nominated their principal as the most supportive (*M* = 3.81, *SD* = 0.50; see Figure 6).

Pastors were also asked what kinds of support or assistance they would be willing to accept from Catholic colleges and universities regarding their current and future needs. Of the choices provided,

Figure 3. Importance of needs pertaining to parish school

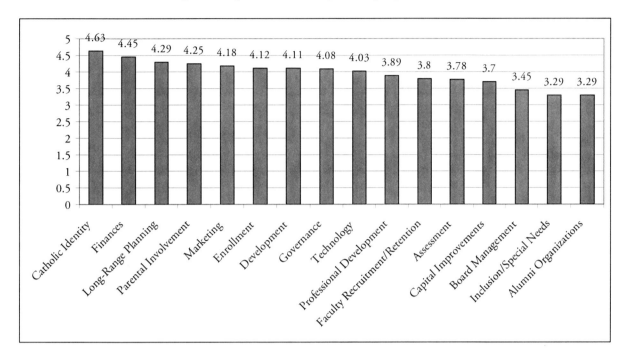

Figure 4. Top areas of need currently addressed by parish school

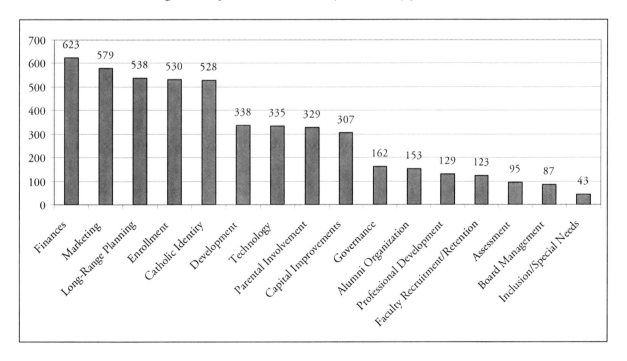

pastors preferred Web-based resources (*n* = 658), diocesan conferences and workshops (*n* = 592), consulting services (*n* = 581), written materials (*n* = 419), regional conferences and workshops (*n* = 415), and university-based conferences and workshops (*n* = 321). Pastors were also able to write-in options that were not included in the prescribed list. First, pastors called for more active engagement and presence of university students in Catholic schools through opportunities such as mentoring, tutoring, and volunteering. Closely related, but distinct because of its more formal nature, pastors

Figure 5. Most reliable source of information at parish school

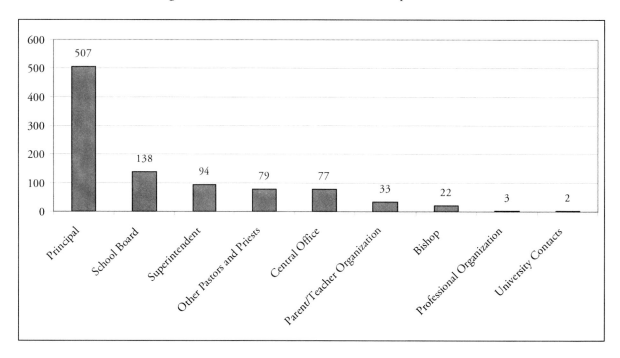

Figure 6. Level of support relating to school matters

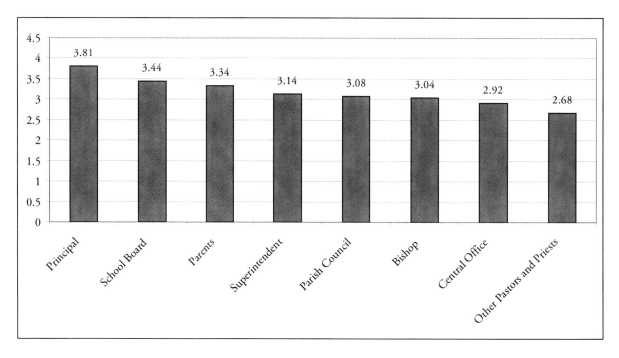

welcomed undergraduate presence in the form of structured internships and as student teachers. Third, pastors cited the possibility of school-university collaboration to support teacher development, continuing education, and ongoing formation for Catholic school teachers.

Although pastors were generally receptive to establishing a working relationship with or accepting assistance from Catholic colleges and universities, very few actually had any discernable relationship with these institutions. The majority of pastors—over 83%—indicated that their school did not have a relationship with a Catholic college or university. More troubling was the finding that 66% of pastors did not perceive the mission of their school to be supported by Catholic institutions of higher education.

> *The majority of pastors—over 83%—indicated that their school did not have a relationship with a Catholic college or university. More troubling was the finding that 66% of pastors did not perceive the mission of their school to be supported by Catholic institutions of higher education.*

Inferential Statistics

Inferential statistics were used to test whether pastors' perceptions of and attitudes toward Catholic schools were significantly different depending on their age, number of years ordained, experience in Catholic schools, and the location of their current parish school (see Table 2, Table 3, Table 5, Table 6, and Table 7 for an overview of variable characteristics). Given the strong loadings revealed via the factor analysis reported above, individual survey items for worth, quality, access, and governance were summed and averaged to provide a composite or factor score for each category for every participant. These data were then used in a multivariate analysis of variance (MANOVA) and yielded statistically significant differences in perceptions and attitudes for three of the four independent variables: age, years ordained, and Catholic school experience (see Table 8). The data revealed that pastor age ($F = 5.33$, $p < .05$), years ordained ($F = 5.33$, $p < .05$), and Catholic school experience ($F = 2.03$, $p < .05$) had a statistically significant effect on perceptions of worth, quality, access, and governance of Catholic schools. No significant difference was detected for location of school. Pairwise contrasts using the Scheffé procedure were conducted and revealed several significant differences among the independent variables.

Age

Pastors who were over 66 years of age, the oldest age category in the sample, reported higher levels of agreement on the quality of Catholic schools than all other age categories except those in the 56-65 age category. Additionally, pastors who were over 66 years of age reported higher levels of agreement regarding the governance of Catholic schools than did any other age category. No significant differences by age were detected for the worth or access of Catholic schools.

Years Ordained

Pastors who were ordained more than 41 years, the category depicting the longest ordination, and pastors who had been ordained 31-40 years reported higher levels of agreement on the worth of Catholic schools than pastors who had been ordained 21-30 years. Pastors ordained from 21 to over 41 years demonstrated higher levels of agreement regarding the quality of Catholic schools than pastors ordained less than 10 years. As with the age category, pastors ordained the longest reported higher levels of agreement with the governance of Catholic schools than any other ordination level except

Table 7

Mean and Standard Deviation for Pastors' Perceptions of and Attitudes Toward Catholic Schools

Factor	Questions	M	SD
Worth	1. The need for Catholic schools is at least as great today as in the past	4.48	0.85
	2. Catholic schools are worth what it costs to operate them	4.22	0.92
	3. Maintaining Catholic schools is an effective use of diocesan and parish resources	4.15	0.94
	4. Catholic schools are an essential part of the Church's educational ministry	4.42	0.81
	5. In addition to the family, Catholic schools are the best means for the religious formation of the young	4.36	0.86
	6. The Catholic school is one of the best means of evangelization in the Church today	4.08	0.98
	7. I enjoy being the pastor of a parish that has a Catholic school	4.34	0.89
Quality	8. Most Catholic schools that I know seem to teach Catholic doctrine reasonably well	3.90	0.87
	9. The Catholic elementary schools that I know have effective programs of religious formation	3.86	0.87
	10. Most Catholic schools that I know seem to have well-prepared and effective teachers	4.08	0.71
	11. Most Catholic schools that I know seem to have a strong Catholic identity	3.93	0.87
	12. Most Catholic schools that I know seem to have well-prepared and effective principals	4.07	0.77
	13. Most Catholic schools that I know seem to have clear goals and priorities	3.83	0.85
Access	14. Every parish should provide some financial support for Catholic schools	4.18	0.99
	15. In areas where there is only one Catholic elementary school and several parishes, each of the parishes should financially support the school	4.37	0.85
	16. The financial support of Catholic schools is the duty of all Catholics whether or not they have children in the schools	4.17	0.97
	17. Some of the surplus of affluent parishes should be shared with financially struggling parishes that support Catholic schools	4.00	1.01
	18. A parish without a Catholic school should financially assist Catholic schools that enroll its students	4.45	0.82
	19. The maintenance of Catholic schools in poor, inner-city areas should be a diocesan priority	4.12	0.89
Governance	20. Parents should have a substantial voice in the governance of Catholic schools	3.64	0.92
	21. Parents must be given a substantial role in the development of policy for Catholic schools	3.62	0.91
	22. All Catholic schools should have school boards/councils	4.39	0.81
	23. When a school serves several parishes, a representative board/council should be responsible for the school's governance	3.95	0.98

those who had been ordained 31-40 years. No significant difference by years ordained was detected for the access of Catholic schools.

Catholic School Attendance

Pastors who attended Catholic schools for at least 3 years reported higher agreement regarding the worth of Catholic schools than did those pastors who did not attend Catholic schools. Similarly, pastors who attended Catholic schools for at least 5 years demonstrated significantly higher agreement on the quality of Catholic schools than pastors who did not attend Catholic schools. No significant differences were detected across levels of Catholic school attendance for the access or governance of Catholic schools.

Table 8
Multivariate and Univariate Analysis of Variance for Independent Variables

	MANOVA	ANOVA			
		Worth	Quality	Access	Governance
Variable	F^a	$F (4, 979)$	$F (4, 978)$	$F (3, 966)$	$F (3, 980)$
Age	5.33*	2.20	14.53*	2.60	8.71*
Years Ordained	5.33*	4.40*	9.44*	1.27	8.27*
Catholic School Experience	2.03*	5.38*	3.31*	2.69	1.90
Location	1.57	0.50	0.79	2.91	2.56

Note. ^{a}F-statistics for the MANOVA were calculated using Pillai's Trace; * $p < .05$

Preliminary analysis of these findings indicates a general trend—pastors with higher age and experience tend to exhibit more positive valuation of Catholic schools. While this assertion does not hold for every derivation of the independent variables, it is certainly evident, and statistically significant, in many of the analyses. Therefore an additional correlation analysis was conducted to determine, in general, the nature of the relationship between age, years ordained, Catholic school attendance, and pastors' perceptions of and attitudes toward Catholic education. Table 9 contains the correlation matrix for this analysis and indicates that there is a significant, positive relationship for nearly every variable. In general, as age, years of ordination, and Catholic school experience increase, so too does the pastor's agreement with the factors representing worth, value, access, and governance of Catholic schools.

Table 9
Correlations for Worth, Quality, Access and Governance of Catholic Schools

Measure	Worth	Quality	Access	Governance
Age	0.08**	0.22**	0.07*	0.17*
Ordained	0.06	0.19**	0.04	0.17**
Attendance	0.11**	0.10**	0.07**	0.07**

Note. ** $p < .01$; * $p < .05$

After the primary data analysis was conducted, several secondary analyses were run to examine additional questions of interest. Actionable variables—those variables that could be addressed or increased through intervention or activity—were explored through a series of factorial and multivariate analyses. These secondary analyses yielded a significant difference for one actionable variable: "Do you perceive the mission of your school to be supported by Catholic institutions of higher education (colleges and/or universities)?"

The results of the analysis in Table 10 indicate that pastors of parishes with schools who perceive the mission of their school to be supported by Catholic institutions of higher education demonstrate

Table 10

Mean, Standard Deviation, and ANOVA for Effect of Perceived University Support

	Support (n = 314)		No Support (n = 616)		ANOVA
	M	SD	M	SD	F (1, 928)
Worth	4.41	0.65	4.23	0.75	13.59*
Quality	4.07	0.58	3.88	0.69	17.65*
Access	4.31	0.66	4.16	0.71	9.34*
Governance	4.01	0.66	3.85	0.67	11.60*

Note. * p < .001

significant, positive increases in their evaluation of the worth, quality, access, and governance of Catholic schools compared to pastors who do not perceive college or university support. This finding is especially poignant considering only 17% of pastors surveyed indicated a partnership with a Catholic institution of higher education. Although not a predictive outcome, these data suggest that Catholic institutions of higher education may play a pivotal role in promoting positive perceptions of and attitudes toward Catholic schools by supporting their mission through university-school partnerships.

Qualitative Findings

Most Important Needs Facing the Parish School

Pastors responded to the item, "In your own words, what are the most important needs facing your parish school in the next two to five years?" Nine hundred seventy-six individual item responses were used in the qualitative analyses. Pastors' responses to this item ranged from 1 to 258 words. In all, 2,134 text segments were identified, coded, and categorized. Table 11 lists each of the 26 themes that emerged from the qualitative data with a brief description and representative quotation for each theme. The 10 themes that emerged beyond the 16 a priori coding categories are italicized in Table 11. Figure 7 depicts the 10 most frequently described needs, listed according to number of coded references to each need area. More detail is provided below for the top five need areas most frequently discussed by the sample.

Enrollment Management

The most frequently mentioned need—cited in 492 text segments—was enrollment management. Of all coded text segments, just over one out of five (23%) dealt with enrollment management. Pastors declared that maintaining and/or increasing student enrollment is the primary pathway for keeping their schools strong and viable. Distilling the needs discussion to its most essential terms, one pastor succinctly stated: "The most basic need is enrollment—we need more students." In answering this question, many simply stated the word "enrollment" or "increase enrollment." Others provided specifics regarding their enrollment difficulties: "Our enrollment has dropped from 400 to 350 in 13 years," and "presently 287 students, 9 years ago, 495 students." In general, successful enrollment management was identified as the "key to vitality."

Other pastors provided more context for their enrollment concerns, for example, addressing enrollment issues as a function of rising costs or increasing tuition: "We need to increase tuition without losing enrollment and pricing ourselves out of business." Similarly, another pastor stated the primary need as "increasing the number of students and the financial stability to meet rising costs of operation." When enrollment challenges were encountered, the impacts were immediate, making it especially challenging "to retain good faculty and maintain a high standard of academic excellence." Despite the challenges, one pastor, emblematic of many, struck a hopeful chord: "To put it simply, the spiraling costs of providing a Catholic education, coupled with a smaller number of participating students, spreads resources too thin for a small parish. Yet, parishioners are willing to make the financial sacrifice."

Table 11
All Coding Categories* with Descriptions, Pastor Needs

Theme	Description	Example Quote
Enrollment Management	Enrollment concerns regarding student recruitment and retention	The most basic need is enrollment; we need more students.
Financial Management	Financial concerns including operating expenses, tuition, and parish subsidy issues	Finance and tuition are always important needs so that money will be available to meet the rising costs.
Maintain Affordability	Expectation that despite rising costs, tuition should remain affordable for all families that desire a Catholic education	To help make Catholic education affordable to those who want it but cannot afford it.
Capital Improvements	Standard maintenance projects, major renovations, and/or new construction/ expansion	Our biggest need is capital improvements as we are preparing to build 10 new classrooms for more space.
Catholic Identity	Faith-filled, practicing environment that deepens knowledge of the faith and one's spiritual growth	I feel the greatest challenge to the Catholic schools is a strong Catholic identity among the faculty and the administration.
Development	Building and cultivating funding resources above and beyond tuition	To grow our educational trust fund to its first-level goal of $1M and use the interest for faculty development and school improvements.
Faculty Recruitment	Identifying, hiring, and retaining qualified Catholic school personnel	Attracting and retaining Catholic faculty is our most difficult challenge.
Miscellaneous	General commentary	We need a discipline policy that is helpful, rather than punitive.
Marketing	Strategies to describe, promote, and increase awareness of Catholic education	Finding a new way to market our mission. Getting prospective families in the doors to see what we offer. Helping people see beyond "bells and whistles" that the public system can afford.
Parish-School Connection	Catholic parish school as an integrated ministry of the parish	Finally, there is a need to create ways to deepen parents' support of the faith formation of their children through their participation in the life of the parish and worship.
Increase Capacity	Expanding physical plant and/or increasing enrollment to meet growing demand	Expanding our facilities to accommodate growth.
Long-Range Planning	Establishing a strategic, visionary plan for the future	We need to further develop a long-range plan which can assure the school's flourishing at a reasonable price for the parish and the parents.
Parent Involvement	Parent voice, input, engagement, and participation in the parish school	Parent involvement and their taking on responsible leadership roles.
Consolidation and Regionalization	Combining and consolidating existing parish schools into new schools and/or regional systems of schools	There are significant issues facing Catholic schools. I do think we will need to go to regional schools rather than just one parish supporting a school. It requires significant resources that make it difficult to support other programs.

Theme	Description	Example Quote
Competition from Other Schools	Competition with other schools (other Catholic, private, or public) in the educational marketplace	To build a proven professional reputation that rivals the "private schools" in town in order to retain our wealthier student base.
Academic Quality	Strong, consistent, documented academic preparation	Encouraging the faculty to be rigorous in the classroom so that the California standards are equaled or surpassed on each grade level. We want our curriculum to be unsurpassed.
School-Level Leadership	Competent school leadership at the building-level, most typically the principal	The need for a solid administrator who can promote the school in the local community, not only as a source of faith formation, but also academic excellence.
Alternative Ways to Evangelize	Consideration of other structures and/or mechanisms to evangelize youth and families that are distinct from Catholic schools	Parishes spend a lot of money and energy on our Catholic school students. We do not see most of these students and their parents in church on Sundays. I wonder how much more effective our parish efforts would be if we could redirect some monies from the Catholic school to parish programs and staff that could do a more effective job of evangelization.
Technology	Use of technology and its applications to enhance education	Modernizing school facilities to keep current with present and future technology.
Parish Subsidy Issues	Issues concerning the nature, amount, and kind of financial support of parish to school	The ability to sustain the school with only the parish supporting it. This is a great financial burden for us.
Alumni Organization	Cultivating a network of graduates to foster support of the alma mater	Effective strategies to awaken the sleeping giant we call the school alumni!
Governance	Leadership/management structures used to direct Catholic schools	Better understanding of board role and relationship to parish.
Professional Development	Ongoing professional training and formation for Catholic school faculty and administrators	Continuing professional development of teachers.
Hispanic Outreach	Efforts to engage Hispanic families in Catholic schools	The increasing Hispanic population, and finding a way to include them in the school, both in terms of convincing them of the importance of education and ways of financing those students who cannot afford the tuition.
Board Management	Strategies to form, develop, and support boards in school governance	Establishment of a consultative school board.
Inclusion and Special Needs	Creating inclusive learning environments and developing systems and resources to best serve children with special needs	Funding of special needs programs.
Assessment	Gauging student academic achievement, needs, proficiency, etc.	Improving the test scores.

*Note. Italicized themes were not part of the a priori coding categories but rather emerged during second-level coding.

Others explained that declining enrollment was a function of changing demographics. Demographic dynamics as they related to enrollment emerged in three forms. First, several cited "changing demographics" in a general way: low birth rates in their area, projected population declines, or a shrinking pool of Catholic youth. For example, one pastor explained that "there simply aren't sufficient children of elementary school age in this older parish." The second trend centered on demographic shifts unique to rural areas. As one pastor from a rural area explained: "The rural population is dwindling. Family farms are becoming extinct and our small towns are drying up with the result that the young are moving to the cities for employment." The third demographic trend focused not on changes in overall population but in the racial and ethnic composition of the area residents: "The neighborhood is changing. We are 99% parishioner attendees but the neighborhood is becoming more and more Asian and less Catholic." It should be noted, too, that pastors often clearly saw the racial and ethnic demographic shifts as pastoral opportunities, citing the need "to respond to the growing population of students who come from Spanish speaking homes who often need special assistance with English language skills."

Figure 7. Ten most frequently coded need areas, ranked by occurrence of coded references

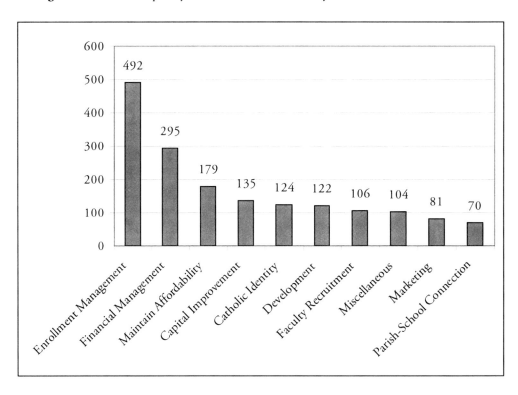

Enrollment was naturally linked to initial student recruitment and ongoing retention. Some pastors maintained that they need to be more aggressive in recruiting, often suggesting that stronger efforts be directed at minorities, particularly Latino families. For example, one noted the need to "increase the percentage of Hispanic students in our school to more reflect the high percentage of our Hispanic parishioners."

Several pastors also mentioned the need to institute PreK programs as a way to recruit students early and build a foundation for long-term retention. Many text segments outlined the need to remain academically competitive in areas with strong and well-regarded public schools. "We are a small rural school located in a very fine public school district. We are very concerned to increase enrollment… and that is difficult since the public school offers a very good option." Maintaining students during the middle school years was also described as a needed area of focus. Pastors seemed to suggest that recruitment and retention are an ongoing process that could be better organized and systematized. As one pastor stated, "Our greatest need is getting students and holding on to them."

Financial Management

The next most frequently discussed need area, with 295 separate text references, was financial management. In their comments concerning the financial management theme, pastors were blunt, direct, and terse. Frequently occurring sample responses included: "cash," "money," "funding," "finances," "fiscal management," "cash flow," "financial viability," "financial stability," "solvency," "economic pressure," and "financial management." One respondent made his point by entering over 200 dollar signs for this survey question. Another commented, "I am sad to say but much comes down to money. We seem to always be talking about that." Similarly, one pastor explained that school financing is the major need in his parish; moreover, he felt that "we don't have a problem that money can't solve—it is the major factor in whether we remain open." According to their open-ended responses, financial management as a central concern touched both longstanding, established schools—"Presently our parish is experiencing a $100,000.00 a year deficit and we need to build a fund to insure the future of the school….Time may run out on us before the next two years,"—and those that were newly established—"We are just 7 months old and face many financial challenges."

In their comments concerning the financial management theme, pastors were blunt, direct, and terse.

Pastors roundly acknowledged that financial health was the driver that determined so much of their school's future. Financial management was deemed critical "to recruit and retain the best faculty, provide technology upgrades, and continue to improve our facilities and curriculum." While adequate financing is clearly required to carry out those positive ends, others described the active neglect that can occur when finances are tight. Two examples were: "much of the maintenance has been deferred to pay teachers and is now showing problems" and "ongoing maintenance is being neglected in order to pay salaries and benefits."

Underscoring the lifeline that a strong financial position lends to a school, pastors used terms like viability and survival when discussing the financial management theme. The simple economics of the situation were placed in stark relief by the comment: "SURVIVAL: With…only 142 students, and a parish population of only 201 families, the school runs a deficit in excess of $100K per year." That comment closely mirrors another respondent's statement: "Survival! Enrollment is about 100 students. The operating deficit is HUGE and we need to refashion the entire school operation so we can keep the school open." One pastor used the phrase "staying alive financially" to describe his major objective over the next few years: "Our financial needs are great. We won't be around in five years if we don't get a big cash source." Since so much is on the line when it comes to money—or the lack of it—pastors' frustration was direct and palpable when discussing this issue:

> It always comes down to this—MONEY! Tuition accounts currently for 1/3 of our income. The rest comes from donations, fundraisers, grants, and liquidation of our assets. Every year we have to liquidate about $40,000 of our assets. In a small school like ours, it's only a matter of time before we're completely strangled.

In reflecting on financial pressures, several pastors conveyed their thoughts on models and/ or approaches to address funding issues. One insight stressed the notion of balanced and integrated funding streams. Three illustrative comments were: "balancing funding between parish support, tuition, and development/fundraising," and "trying to balance financial commitments from school parents and from the parish," and "we need to raise funds, receive grants, etc. to help with finances and capital improvement."

Maintain Affordability

The third most frequently occurring need area, maintaining affordability, was addressed in 179 separate text segments. It is especially important to note that this category emerged via open coding of pastors' survey responses and was not one of the original 16 a priori coding categories. This indicates the particular salience of this theme since pastors actively provided information on this topic even though it was not listed among the response set of the previous question (which could have had a priming influence on open-ended responses).

Review of pastors' comments about maintaining affordability revealed the decisive proposition that Catholic schools must maintain affordability for any and all families that desire such education for their children. The notion of affordability for all was exemplified by comments such as the need to "keep the skyrocketing

One pastor maintained that "we must first be a Catholic school rather than a private school."

cost of Catholic education affordable for everyone who wants it," and "making our school affordable for families of all economic levels," and "continuing to maintain a reasonable tuition rate that will allow low to middle income families to continue to send their children to our school." If costs are not controlled, some expressed concern that Catholic schools may price themselves out of the market.

Closely related to school affordability for all income levels was the fear expressed by pastors regarding what the alternative might look like. That is, Catholic schools must not become the province solely of the affluent. Pastors were vehement in stating that if tuition is not approachable for a wide range of parents, the result will be schools "just for the wealthy" or "a private upper caste school." Pastors spoke about keeping tuition affordable to the "middle class person," or the "population with a middle class/moderate income." Several cautioned that Catholic schools are already becoming elitist, sometimes embracing a private school identity that should be avoided. One pastor maintained that "we must first be a Catholic school rather than a private school." Still other respondents warned that ensuring equal access via affordable tuition has particular import for minority families: "Making the school available to all who wish to come—especially the Latino population. It's an ongoing challenge in a predominantly affluent Anglo community to see that it does not become a rich kids' academy."

Catholic school tuition affordability also was discussed in relation to competing with local public schools for students, directly influencing enrollment and retention. Balancing the need for tuition increases—and its concomitant impact on families—takes on yet another dimension when a "highly rated public school" is a good option. Meeting the "cost of education at a Catholic school in a city where the public schools are very good" is a daunting proposition for many families that struggle financially. One pastor confirmed that "tuition for our school is prohibitive for some, especially with a strong public school system that offers so many programs for families free."

In response to the affordability issue, the pastors spoke about the need to establish systems of scholarships, aid, and financial assistance for students and their families. One pastor cited that as his primary need:

> The most important would be to be able to fund those families who would like to send their children to the school but have REAL financial issues. Need to establish some sort of fund to allow current parish support to be used in the area of scholarships instead of going to supplement the current tuition structure.

Pastors described the need to be creative and to develop innovative structures to fund these efforts. Some advocated endowments to keep tuition down, support needy students, and make teachers' salaries competitive. Another mentioned an ongoing commitment to fostering the school's own foundation to provide assistance over the long term.

A final sub-theme within the affordability issue was the recognition by some that the current affordability challenges are due in no small part to a regional and national economic downturn. One pastor explained that "the parents are being squeezed financially—higher living costs, increases in tuition, but not a sufficient increase in salary." Some cited specific changes in their local economic base, which in turn exerts an effect on demographic shifts. For example, one noted, "being in a small town that just lost two major businesses, the economic climate is such that parents are questioning if they can afford tuition."

Interrelationship Among the First Three Themes

After consideration of the first three themes, it should be noted that while each was presented independently, they are highly overlapping in nature. For example, it appears impossible to talk about enrollment management without citing financial concerns. These two themes were clearly two sides of the same coin. One respondent stated, "We must improve our financial situation. The biggest driver for our finances is enrollment. If we increase enrollment, we will improve the finances." Likewise, the symbiotic relationship of enrollment and finances was demonstrated by the following comments: "The need to deal with declining numbers of students and increasing costs at the same time," and "the financial stability of the school depends on a significant increase in enrollment." When considering the dynamic interplay of enrollment and finances, the third theme—concerns about parents' ability to afford Catholic education—consequently came to the forefront. As an example, the following comment illustrates a precarious balance, showing the complex interrelationship among these themes and closely approximating the day-to-day reality of enrollment, finances, and affordability: "[We need] more pupils, with a concomitant realization on parents' part of value of a Catholic education…

[that will] keep the enrollment consistent so financial concerns will not be overbearing to our parents, especially in increasing tuition."

Capital Improvements

Capital improvements were discussed via 135 coded text segments, making it the fourth most frequently described need area of surveyed pastors. Pastors' comments regarding capital improvements were grouped into four categories. First, one group of pastors described the deteriorating condition of buildings and physical plants that were extremely old, in some cases over a century since their initial construction. For example, one pastor referenced multiple buildings on the parish property dating to 1872, 1930, 1955, and 1991—all needing capital improvements. Across all responses, specific improvements mentioned were heating and air conditioning upgrades, refurbished athletics facilities, updated lighting, new roofing, boiler replacement, and catching up on deferred maintenance. One respondent offered this piece of advice for staying one step ahead of capital improvements: "Maintain the building and not even consider deferring maintenance. This includes trying to do things right the first time and not taking the most inexpensive route, no matter how tempting." A second group of pastors reported that their primary capital improvement projects over the next few years would be centered on facility expansion. Some described expanding the existing physical plant to meet current needs or projected growth: "We are preparing to build 10 new classrooms for more space." Others explained that they were adding new buildings to the property to house classrooms, specialized classrooms (media centers, science or computer labs, etc.), a library, and/or a gymnasium. The third category of capital improvement reflects pastors representing schools that either just have or will soon embark on building new facilities altogether. One described building a new school and youth formation center, another is building a new school because the old one was too small and inaccessible, and one is focused on "completion of a new 55,000 sq. ft. state of the art facility." Two pastors described their new building projects as being prompted by increased enrollments, driven in one case by a new PreK program and in the other by growth in a nearby military base. The fourth category includes those that described capital improvements as an instrumental strategy to achieve other goals, like boosting enrollment and remaining unique in a competitive market. For example, after outlining a list of improvement projects including roof repair, a new library, media lab and a science facility, the pastor explained, "These are our greatest needs in order to compete with our local public school system which is considered very good."

Catholic Identity

Rounding out the top five most referenced need areas, Catholic identity was discussed via 124 coded text segments. One concise comment captured the essence of why this need area was so salient among all other areas: "None of it is worthwhile unless we maintain strong Catholic identity." The pastors indicated that Catholic identity is so central because it is, above all, the primary mechanism for transmission of the Catholic faith. Pastors referenced faith transmission on at least two levels. First, they described the direct faith development that schools foster among youth:

Our greatest concern is to address the spiritual needs of our children, drawing them into a deeper experience of their Catholic faith, drawing them closer to Jesus and Mother Mary, so that they can live their faith for the rest of their lives.

In some cases, pastors clarified that the expression and fostering of Catholic identity occurred among students who were not Catholic, and that schools needed to be responsive to that need. For example, one pastor defined his greatest need as "evangelizing a population that is largely students of other faiths." Second, many responses described intergenerational faith transmission, most often between parents and youth: "Making sure that we identify and live out our mission…to help parents pass on the faith to their children." Another expressed the importance of "having parents practice the Catholic faith and be more involved in their child's learning of the Catholic faith."

Another sub-theme regarding Catholic identity emerged strongly in pastors' descriptions of the need for a clearer relationship between the parish and the school. Pastors felt that a more fully developed Catholic identity strengthens the ministry of the school in its parish context, creating an ethos of unity and common mission. In light of such observations, pastors articulated the need to "deepen our Catholic identity and spirituality" by making "a further effort to involve Catholic parents in Sunday liturgy with their children." Parish life would be enhanced and enlivened by stable connections between church and school, undergirded by a unifying Catholic identity. One pastor elaborated that he will continue "to advance the understanding among all parishioners that the school is part of our parish mission and Catholic identity as a whole and we need to collectively own the parish school and not simply 'rent' it when we have need of it."

> *Pastors felt that a more fully developed Catholic identity strengthens the ministry of the school in its parish context, creating an ethos of unity and common mission.*

Many survey responses extolled the fact that Catholic identity is paramount to the unique nature of Catholic schools. Pastors were adamant that Catholic schools are not merely private schools. Moreover, it appeared that they often needed to remind parents of that fact: "Another issue which we must focus on is the Catholic identity. We have parents who want to see our school as a private school and not to incorporate Catholic values." Similarly, another added that his main goal was "keeping the school open and Catholic, with all that this entails, especially the practice of the Catholic faith by participating families." In other words, Catholic identity and values are the defining elements that separate the parish school from its private school counterparts. Consequently, when parents are discerning their children's education pathway, pastors want the motivation to be sending "their children to the school primarily for a Catholic education rather than a private education."

Pastors made several comments describing how critical it is that Catholic identity be strongly and deeply embraced among school faculty. They expressed that without an abiding sense of Catholic identity, the faculty could not successfully combine high quality education with students' faith formation. One pastor's desire was a school populated with "qualified faculty who are imbued with the Catholic spirit and bring it to their students." Another seconded this idea but clarified that faculty often cannot grow in faith alone and unaided. He suggested that "we need to sort of help the faculty to be better and deeper people of faith."

General Comments from Pastors

Pastors responded to Question 33, "Please provide any additional comments regarding thoughts and opinions on Catholic schools and Catholic school leadership." Four hundred forty-four individual responses were used in the qualitative analyses for this item. Pastors' responses ranged from 2 to 451

Table 12
All Coding Categories with Descriptions, Open-Ended Pastor Commentary

Theme	Description	Example Quote
Catholic Identity	Faith-filled, practicing environment that deepens knowledge of the faith and one's spiritual growth	We are focusing on ensuring a strong Catholic identity in the school in the face of an increasing number of families who do not practice their faith.
Financial Management	Financial concerns including operating expenses, tuition, and parish subsidy issues	Financing the parish is very difficult and has been the hardest part of serving as pastor in a rural parish with a small school.
Valuing Catholic Schools	Supportive comments regarding Catholic schools	Catholic schools are a valuable resource for evangelization and parish life.
Leadership	Calls for improved school, parish, diocesan, and broader Church leadership for Catholic schools	Our schools do not seem to be attracting qualified and creative people to be leaders (i.e., principals). There is a lack of vision and an unwillingness on the part of many pastors and administrators to find new ways of governing Catholic schools.
School Families Must Attend Sunday Mass	Catholic school parents and students must be faith-filled, practicing, and visible parishioners	The biggest problem facing Catholic schools is the growing number of Catholics that do not practice their faith.
General Governance	Issues regarding the overall leadership and/or management of Catholic schools	As long as accountability in the Church remains drawn as it is now, I think policy and governance must be heavily in the hands of the pastor and principal.
Parish-School-Parent Connections	The interrelationships between the parish, the school, and parent involvement in each	I need parents to be more involved in parish life and see a connection between school and Catholic life.
Survey Comments or Clarifications	Respondent commentary regarding survey construction and/or clarifying their responses to specific items	Thank you for undertaking this survey and thanks for giving me the chance to participate.
Consolidation or Regionalization	Combining and consolidating existing parish schools into new schools and/ or regional systems of schools	My parish is part of a multi-parish school. I believe this is the best option for the future of elementary Catholic education. This model should be given much more consideration. The traditional parochial school model needs to be re-thought to remain vital, competitive, and balanced.
Alternative Ways to Evangelize	Consideration of other structures and/or mechanisms to evangelize youth and families that are distinct from Catholic schools	It is the responsibility of the Church to provide religious education for its faithful, but that does not have to be done through Catholic schools. The religious education system can work just as well.

Theme	Description	Example Quote
Ensuring Access and Affordability	Expectation that despite rising costs, tuition should remain affordable for all families that desire a Catholic education	It is becoming more difficult to raise the funds needed for quality education. It is difficult to keep the costs at a level where the majority of the people can attend a Catholic school.
Faculty Issues	Issues regarding faculty characteristics, professional development, adequate compensation, etc.	Catholic schools are notoriously unjust with wages for the staff and educators. Whatever can be done to assist just wages or provide ongoing formation will help their morale.
Parent Role in Governance	Detailing the specific roles of parents in school governance	Parents should have a voice. However, it may be difficult for a parent to see the larger picture. That is why the ultimate decision should fall with the pastor, his principal, and when necessary the school council.
Inner-City Schools and Serving the Poor	Focused on Catholic schools' serving the poor in inner-city contexts	Catholic education in the inner city is key. It is the Catholic Church's great gift to the community, even when there are not a great number of Catholics.
Questioning the Value of Catholic Schools	Neither positively nor negatively weighted comments that question the overall value of Catholic schools	Catholic schools remain a very important part of the Church's mission, but must always remain aware of the many other needs of the parishes in which they reside. While not the school's fault, they can drain resources so heavily, as to make fulfilling the mission of the parish at large very difficult. Catholic schools must always remain aware of the needs of the larger Catholic community that gives them their life and support.
Pastor as Key	Citing the pastor as integral and indispensable to the success of the parish school	Pastors who wish to have a Catholic school should be assigned to such a parish. If the pastor is not interested nor able, he should be given another assignment. The pastor needs to be a key player in the future of Catholic schools. The schools cannot be given over to principals. The parish model necessitates the involvement, support, direction and enthusiasm of the pastor.
Negative View of Catholic Schools	Negative commentary on Catholic schools	Catholic schools came about in the 19th century because the public school system was blatantly anti-Catholic. It was a Protestant institution. The situation has changed long, long ago. I think we'd do better today to focus on improving our public schools and our religious education programs.
Enrollment	Enrollment concerns regarding student recruitment and retention	It is important to keep our Catholic schools, but the cost factor is way out of control. Our enrollment is going down and costs go up.
Miscellaneous	General comments	Though I am happy to be a pastor with a school now, I can see this changing as I get older. In a few years I will no longer want the extra involvement that comes with having a school.
Pastor Training/ Development	Citing specific training, formation, and/or professional development needs for pastors with Catholic schools	Many pastors have been given virtually no preparation in regard to faith formation of young people, much less the operation of a Catholic school.

words. In all, 723 text segments were identified, coded, and categorized. Open coding revealed 20 themes inherent in the data. These are listed in Table 12 with brief descriptions and sample quotations. Figure 8 depicts the 10 most frequently described themes, listed according to number of coded references to each theme. More detail is provided below for the five general themes most frequently discussed by the sample and Appendix B provides additional narrative description for themes 6 through 10.

Figure 8. Ten most frequently coded open-ended response themes, ranked by occurrence of coded references.

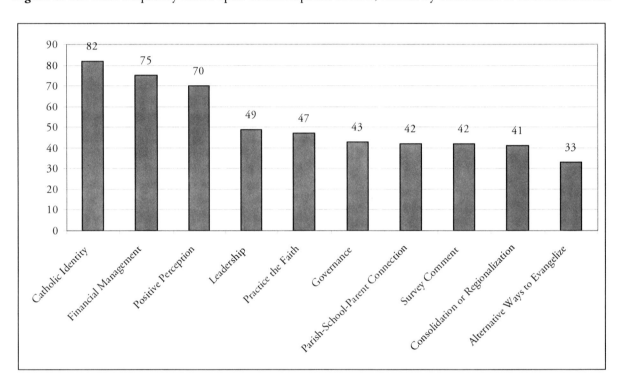

Embracing Catholic Identity and Instilling the Faith

Paralleling its importance in the first qualitative item about needs, Catholic identity was the most frequently mentioned theme, cited in 82 text segments. Pastors posited that if Catholic education is to truly be a faith experience, students, families, and the broader parish community must deeply embrace a pervasive Catholic identity. That contention was the sine qua non of the successful parish school: "If we lose our Catholic identity we lose our schools," and "a strong Catholic identity in our schools is more important than ever."

Many pastors insisted that the Catholic school is not just a private school, but all too often it is perceived as such. In many markets, Catholic schools are envisioned as a private school option, rather than a faith-based, religious school, prompting one pastor to remark, "Many parents want the discipline, safety, and technology more than the Gospel orientation." One respondent asserted that if it is "merely a building with a cross on it where everyone learns how to be 'nice' to everybody else with some vague religious sentiment added, we are not dealing with a Catholic school." Another pastor offered this articulate perspective:

It is essential that any Catholic school be truly Catholic. If the Catholic identity of a school (in catechesis, liturgy, morality, and service) is lacking, then the school ceases to serve its primary function. Catholic schools do not exist to offer a private educational experience or more generically to simply offer another approach to education. Rather, Catholic schools must have Christ at the center of their identity and mission. With such an identity, a close relationship to Christ's Church also naturally flows.

Some pastors contended that parents use Catholic schools to escape their flawed local public system while others enroll their children at the parish school seeking nothing more than the cheapest private school option. Despite the sense that parents and others may blur the distinction between private and Catholic education, one pastor remained adamant, "I object to running a private school; I run a Catholic school."

Another notion that surfaced in regard to Catholic identity was the sense that it is progressively eroding. One respondent lamented that some schools now have "a Catholic identity in name only." Catholic identity, according to some, does not have a strong valence among competing priorities:

There is a loss of a sense of Church since the families are focusing on just the education. Their priority is the academic excellence, the discipline, the safe environment for learning and growth, the athletics and extracurricular activities and then, if there is any room, faith, and maybe Catholic faith, if there is time.

Furthermore, several pastors questioned whether Catholic schools are effectively instilling the faith and in doubting schools' overall efficacy, they claimed not to value them as much as they once did.

Several observations were forwarded as to why schools are lacking in Catholic identity and pinpointed why faith transmission is not as effective as it could be. First, pastors cited the declining numbers of Catholic faculty in some schools as a direct challenge that undermines Catholic identity. Second, multiple responses discussed the need for school faculty to receive deeper and more comprehensive faith background themselves: "I think the faith formation taking place in the classroom is not strong enough because our teachers are not well trained, and the younger teachers do not have a strong faith practice background." Another claimed that "the principals and teachers often do not know the true faith or educate in the true faith." A solution offered by one pastor was that "workshops and inservice on Catholic identity should be required of all who wish to teach or be administrators in Catholic schools." A third strand of comments clustered around the idea that the presence of consecrated religious in schools would augment their Catholicity. One representative statement noted that

"If we lose our Catholic identity we lose our schools."

We still lack the Catholic identity we had when more religious women and men and priests were actively involved in schools. I find that many well intentioned lay teachers still lack sufficient formation to instill the kind of fervor for the faith and Catholic ambiance that is needed.

Financial Management

In line with the major emergent themes relating to needs, 75 text segments for the open-ended item dealt with financial management. Pastors frequently used the words "difficult" or "challenging" when describing school finances. Others were more vehement in their commentary: "It is important to keep our Catholic schools, but the cost factor is way out of control." Financial concerns centered on achieving a balance between school operating costs, parish contribution, and tuition: "The challenge is to find a way to make it economically feasible to keep tuition reasonable and parish subsidization manageable." In dealing with financial challenges, pastors sometimes felt isolated, as exemplified by the following excerpt:

> Pastors can't do it all anymore. Bishops have other irons in the fire. Parents are busy. We expect too much from volunteers—run the candy sale, Market Day, develop an alumni database, organize the festival, direct mail alums. We need professionals—educated and trained—to help grow the business/financial side of parishes and schools. I can't run a million dollar campaign with volunteers, no matter how nice they are.

Some expressed that schools are heavy burdens on the parish: "Money is a huge concern for the relationship of schools and parishes. I may have to let the school go, despite its many years of service, to keep the parish alive." Others maintained that "a school kills any other ministries in most parishes. They are a huge drain on parish budgets," and "they are very quickly consuming an undue portion of parish personnel and financial resources and are serving a smaller and smaller percentage of Catholic families and youth." Another noted, "I think we have a great school, awesome faculty and great parents, but the underlying gorilla is still trying to finance the school while also maintaining the programs of the parish." One respondent likened schools to "financial black holes (absorbing every dollar you could conceivably put into them)."

Much pastor commentary focused on the proportion of resources that parishes contribute to school operations. Many cited the percentage of resources that support the school: "In this diocese parishes contribute 60+% of school operating budgets," "71% of my parish income goes to support Catholic education," "the school is a quarter of a million dollars in debt, and 40% of the parish budget is spent on the school." Pastors often wrote that there should be a "more equitable division of the funds available from the Sunday parish collection." Similarly, one explained that "parishes like mine put all their money into the subsidy and have nothing left for anything else. We need to have a more balanced approach regarding assets available to the parish as a whole." Aligned with that same sentiment, one said, "We cannot continue to budget the majority of our monies to Catholic schools when other aspects of faith formation are also in need of development and monies." One pastor's heartfelt statement expressed:

> I am soul-weary from financially subsidizing our parochial school. It is an injustice to the vast majority of worshipping parishioners that half of the offertory collection goes to support the just salary of my Catholic school teachers....My whole life boils down to this: completely bankrupting the parish for the sake of 181 kids out of a parish of 1,100 families.

Given the serious financial concerns raised by pastors, they were not without suggestions for alterative strategies to support Catholic schools. A few mentioned moving to a "full stewardship model of parish life—no tuition, but all parishioners challenged to practice 5% financial stewardship toward the parish." One contingent stressed that, where feasible, schools should transition to a "cost to educate" tuition model. "I believe the funding of a child's education is the responsibility of the parents and that a Catholic school's finances should be funded by the tuition without the finances coming from the parish offertory giving." Another group emphasized the importance of founding, structuring, and building stable, profitable endowments and thereby leaving behind the "nickel and dime approach to fundraising." Consolidation and regionalization of parish schools was mentioned as a viable strategy to alleviate financial pressures: "The model of one parish supporting and providing one school will not work in many cases. It will be necessary to use a system approach to providing Catholic schools." One predicted that regional schools are the solution for the future and another proffered a model whereby dioceses establish a "Catholic school fund or system and every parish should put money into the fund regardless if they have a school or not and then every school should be allotted needed monies per capita somewhat like the public school system." A final category of financial suggestions were those that stressed the notion of creativity—finding new and innovative financial solutions. These ideas included more pronounced partnerships with universities, more aggressive grant writing and grant-seeking, cultivating corporate support, and enlisting foundation support.

Valuing Catholic Schools

Positive views of Catholic schools were expressed in 70 text segments. Several pastors used the open-ended item simply to comment on their positive view of the mission and ministry of Catholic schools. Many proclaimed that they have been, and will continue to be, staunch advocates for Catholic schools. Those pastors embraced their ministry in schools. For example, one wrote: "I am proud of this apostolate of the Catholic Church and I am delighted that I am a pastor who has care of a Catholic elementary school!" Others wrote that "Catholic education is our most valuable resource and must be maintained at any cost," and it is "essential to the mission of the Church." Responses under this rubric of positive perception were peppered with phrases like "well worth it," "great gift," "a valuable resource," "do much good," "great asset," "absolutely essential," "source of life," and "wonderful treasure." Succinctly, one commented, "The future of the Church is in Catholic education."

One sub-theme of positive perceptions was that the Catholic school was a vital part of holistic and vibrant parish life. "Our school adds greatly to the life of our parish," a pastor wrote, noting that "Mass with the school children remains one of the highlights of the week." Schools were referred to as a life-giving, integral, and community-focused component of the parish family. Parishes grow strong—and are continually energized—through the presence of a school. One pastor envisioned the school as a necessary and complementary element for families' overall growth in the faith: "The work and mission of the family, the parish church, and the parish school must be clearly defined. All three sectors have their respective role in the living of the faith."

Schools were referred to as a life-giving, integral, and community-focused component of the parish family. Parishes grow strong—and are continually energized—through the presence of a school.

Some saw the role of Catholic schools as one of even heightened importance given our current sociohistorical milieu. One said that "education and formation in the Catholic faith and culture is extremely important for our youth today, faced with a world that is becoming more and more materialistic and humanistic." Similarly, another respondent affirmed his belief in Catholic schools "especially in the materialistic and sexually explicit environment we currently live in here in America." Still another suggested that "given the culture and society in which we live, Catholic schools are perhaps more important now than ever before in building the Kingdom of God in this world."

Another positive view of Catholic schools sees them as powerful agents of change and support for the poor as well as mechanisms for community revitalization. A pastor observed that

> Andrew Greeley's research has shown that Catholic schools have been the best instrument of all Church and government institutions in the history of our country in moving more people out of poverty and into the middle class than any other. They have also helped build up the Church in America. I think our schools still have that role to play in both of these areas.

In close accord with the above comment, a pastor of an inner-city school was convinced of the life-changing role of his Catholic school. He explained that

> in many places the Catholic school provides an environment that is relatively free of the fear of gangs, drugs, and violence and is conducive to a quality education….Catholic schools can provide a family for many students who have very little family structure and support at home. By integrating faith with life in all classes and school activities, and teaching students how they can develop a loving relationship with God and others, they can learn to love the Church as their own family.

Other comments echoed these selections and showed the firm commitment that Catholic schools can still be invaluable tools of evangelization in the inner city and among the poor. Even with the challenges facing some inner-city schools, the conviction of one pastor was emblematic of many: "I'll go down fighting to keep it open because it does serve the poor and I believe our Lord Jesus Christ calls us to serve the poor."

Leadership

The next most frequently occurring theme among the open-ended responses, with 49 text segments, was leadership. Strong leadership in support of Catholic schools is needed. Pastors evoked the call for leadership on several different levels. First, pastors cited the importance of school-based leadership, most typically embodied in the role of the principal. Without a competent, faith-filled individual at the helm, the success of the parish school is in jeopardy. They noted that "the presence of well-educated and well-formed principals is essential to the life of a school," and "good administrators that empower their faculty and staff are the key to success in this generation of Catholic schools." One pastor's ideal leadership description came through in this comment: "We need strong principals who are loving, kind, gentle, friendly, and dynamic and are faithful to the magisterium." Articulating the ideal set of qualities does not ensure that such an individual is easily identified, however. One pastor said that "well trained and well formed principals are very difficult to find." Another noted, "I have had some very good principals, and very poor principals. There doesn't seem to be much middle ground." In sum, though, respondents felt that having a well-qualified principal is key; pastors need "a leader who can build community through communication—listening to hopes and needs and speaking a clear direction for all to follow."

Without a competent, faith-filled individual at the helm, the success of the parish school is in jeopardy.

Second, effective and proactive diocesan leadership was called for, especially for particular initiatives. Regarding parish mergers and consolidations, one pastor explained that "Our diocese provides little initiative for consolidation of small or failing schools. There is a feeling among pastors that we are left hanging about such initiatives." In another diocese facing school closings, the pastor remarked that "the local bishop must engage in planning and studies to facilitate this type of amalgamation and needs to be the voice of reason and strength when it comes to making decisions about closure and consolidation." Others said that diocesan leadership would be especially helpful in assisting schools with financial matters. For example, one pastor cited the need for a diocesan-wide approach to building a Catholic school endowment. Another pastor from a diocese with declining Catholic schools explained, "Most of them are struggling because the population has shifted. There is no strategic plan to deal with this so it looks like many of the schools will die. We need a leader who can help come up with a plan." On the positive side, a pastor recounted that his diocesan office had been particularly supportive during a school restructuring: "The central office is offering tremendous guidance and leadership in this project."

Third, many pastors yearned for stronger leadership from bishops and diocesan offices evinced through a broader, more comprehensive vision. One needed more outright signs of backing: "More vocal support of Catholic education from our bishops would be appreciated." Some saw the need to reiterate a clearly defined purpose: "The leadership needs to set the vision of why the schools exist and see that the mission and procedures are in line with that." One pastor hoped for guidance: "There needs to be a unifying plan or vision from the bishop of the diocese to create interdependence among all diocesan grade schools and parishes." In some cases, pastors felt unsupported, as portrayed in the comment, "Although our archdiocese states that it has a strong commitment to Catholic education, there is virtually no long-term planning and even less consultation. It is almost as if the archdiocese is waiting for the system to collapse before it admits to the crisis." In a similar vein, one remarked pointedly, "The bishops and diocesan office have too much going on elsewhere to pay close attention to my school and parish until there are major problems and it is too late."

In asserting a new vision for schools, pastors highlighted several key variables: more resources, renewed strategic commitment, and creativity. One suggested that "there is a lack of vision and an unwillingness on the part of many pastors and administrators to find new ways of governing schools. We need a bold new vision of what the mission of Catholic elementary education really is." Stressing the need for a channeling of existing resources, a pastor said: "Bishops and dioceses need to support Catholic schools. It is not just a parish need. Catholic schools provide much needed Catholic lifelong formation." One pastor was concise in describing the gravity of the situation; he asserted that "I can't begin to tell you how important Catholic schools are at this moment for the Church and for the future. More diocesan resources need to be set aside for strategic planning for Catholic schools."

School Families Need to Attend Sunday Mass

In 42 text segments, pastors expressed strong opinions about the need for Catholic school families to more fully embrace and practice the faith. One overarching comment summarized this viewpoint: "We need a community that truly practices the faith if we're to have Catholic schools." Numerous responses mirrored this one: "There is a concern among many pastors of parishes with Catholic schools that the children do not participate in Sunday Masses due to the fact that their parents do not." While certainly recognizing the school as an instrument of evangelization, pastors can only meet parents halfway. That is, as summarized by one pastor, "The problem with today's school children is the lack of commitment to the practice of the faith by parents. A school is able to no more than reinforce the faith that is first formed in the family." Responses aligning with this theme overlapped greatly with the Catholic identity theme, especially the notion that some parents see the school as a private option rather than a Catholic school. One pastor described it thusly: "They see the school as a way to give their children a good education and prepare for college and give them some good values. Unfortunately, they don't see any need to teach their children at home or to come to church on a regular basis."

"Ask any pastor what percentage of families from the school attend Sunday Mass, and the answer will be shockingly low," one pastor wrote. Many respondents attempted to quantify just how many do not attend Mass: "approximately 35% of the parents do not seem to see the need for weekly worship," "close to 80 percent do not attend Sunday Mass," "45% of our children and parents do not attend Mass regularly," and "70%…do not practice the faith that we seek to instill." Regardless of the actual number, perhaps one pastor settled on an apt conclusion when he noted, "Most pastors I know are appalled that children and families of the parochial school do not show up regularly for Mass on weekends."

There was a trend among responses indicating that pastors were essentially using the yardstick of Mass attendance to judge the effectiveness of Catholic schools. The logic is simple: If Catholic schools exist primarily as tools of evangelization, is it not fair to assess their efficacy by how many children and families are in the pews each Sunday? One outlined such a position:

I wonder about the effectiveness of Catholic schools in Catholic formation—a high percentage of students do not regularly attend Mass because their families do not attend Mass. I do wonder if the financial and personnel resources of parishes are better spent in comprehensive religious education.

Another wondered "how much more effective our parish efforts would be if we could redirect some monies from the Catholic school to parish programs and staff that could do a more effective job of evangelization." Some asserted that students attending public schools are more likely to be present at Mass and that public schools are just as good for cultivating vocations. Still others were not sure that Catholic schools are achieving their goal of "teaching the faith and forming Catholics. If not, we have to change or get out of the education business."

Summary of Major Findings

The Notre Dame Study of U.S. Pastors employed a mixed-method survey design to examine the needs and dispositions of over 1,000 pastors with regard to their leadership in Catholic schools. The study builds on previous scholarship by J. S. O'Brien (1986, 1987) and Convey (1999) with the primary goal to understand the needs of pastors in relationship to Catholic education and then to formulate an action plan to meet those needs. Through this endeavor we affirm that the pastor holds a uniquely important leadership role in the parish and in the Catholic school, so important that no effort to serve Catholic schools can succeed without them.

Faith, Finances, and the Future is a detailed report of the major methodological features and salient findings of the study. This title reflects the two major needs that emerged from the quantitative and qualitative analysis of pastors' responses. Below is a general overview of these findings.

Finances

Pastors indicated a triumvirate of financial concerns they felt were important to their school, were currently being addressed in their schools, and were likely to be the most important needs facing their schools in the next 2 to 5 years: enrollment management, financial management, and affordability. Financial management and enrollment were ranked first and fourth, respectively, out of a list of 16 possible needs currently being addressed by the parish school. Analysis of pastors' free response to the question revealed that enrollment, financial management, and affordability were the three most frequently cited concerns facing parish schools. The interconnection of these themes is characterized through pastors' statements imploring the "need to deal with declining numbers of students and increasing costs at the same time," and recognizing that "the financial stability of the school depends on a significant increase in enrollment."

Faith

The second major theme to emerge from the data reflected pastors' concern regarding the Catholic identity of their parish schools. Catholic identity was ranked fifth out of a list of 16 possible needs currently being addressed by the parish school. Catholic identity was also the first in that list not related to financial management. In a qualitative analysis of pastors' free response to that same question, Catholic identity was also the fifth most frequently cited response. Pastors' concern with the unique identity of their schools was succinctly stated by one pastor who said, "None of it is worthwhile unless we maintain strong Catholic identity."

University School Partnerships

Analysis of pastors' perceptions and attitudes toward Catholic schools uncovered an alarming statistic. Nearly 70% of all pastors did not perceive the mission of their schools to be supported by Catholic institutions of higher education. Furthermore, those who did perceive support from Catholic institutions of higher education reported higher, positive agreement with the worth, quality, access, and governance of Catholic schools. What is most troubling, then, is that only 17% of pastors indicated that their school currently had a partnership with a Catholic institution of higher education.

Recommendations

The insights, observations, and concerns of pastors reported in this study provide a fertile knowledge base for ongoing reflection and action on behalf of Catholic schools. Knowing that the challenges of pastors are heavily focused in the areas of finance and faith, our recommendations flow broadly from these two categories. In an effort to synthesize the data generated from this study and identify strategic initiatives for the immediate future, we use these two categories to delve deeper into the insights of pastors, affirm their lived experience, and build a foundation for a systemic response to their manifest needs.

Finances and faith could easily be understood as secular versus sacred challenges. Fundraising, enrollment management, institutional advancement, and debt reduction are activities clearly on the business side of educational administration and include budgetary issues common to many schools, public and private. The faith questions identified by pastors involve the Catholic identity both of the school and its stakeholders. Full and active participation in parish life, in the parish school and beyond, is overwhelmingly a major concern for pastors. Thus, while pastors often struggle to pay the bills and meet budget, they have an equally pressing and concomitant pastoral concern for the faith formation of the families they serve. Pastors want to run fiscally solvent parishes and schools, but they also want the Catholic faith to be a living, important, dynamic element in the lives of parish families. They want to see that Jesus Christ makes a difference in the lives of the people they serve and they want the schools to be instruments of evangelization as well as education.

In delineating recommendations for the areas of finance and faith, it would be easy to compartmentalize the two as separate and equal areas of concern, the secular question of finances and the sacred question of Catholic identity. As we shall see, these two categories can be understood as a manifestation of a single challenge facing the Catholic community, albeit one with many nuances.

Recommendations in the Area of Finances

Financial administrators often simplify complex budgetary matters by reviewing income and expenses for shareholders, hoping to focus attention on decreasing expenses while increasing revenue. Our recommendations in the area of finance follow the same structure.

Decreasing Expenses
When fiscal challenges emerge, a major error in business and industry as well as education is to look

for new sources of revenue without an equally hard look at decreasing expenses. Raising tuition, as any seasoned Catholic school administrator can attest, does not guarantee any increased revenue. On paper the budget may show increased anticipated revenue and a balanced situation, but steep tuition increases more often than not result in decreased enrollment (DeLuca, 2001).

Catholic schools can help their financial situations by working to decrease expenses. The most important expense line item in need of national attention is health care. With the exception of the dioceses in the state of Michigan and four dioceses in Texas (Healey, 2008), every diocese in the United States pays retail for health care insurance for their employees—priests, pastors, principals, teachers, pastoral ministers, and musicians. Every diocese negotiates its own plan, creates its own insurance group for coverage, and thereby fails to take advantage of the national reach of the U.S. Church and the economy of scale to be gained by uniting into regional plans or one national, comprehensive plan. It is not an exaggeration to suggest that the U.S. Catholic Church is leaving millions of dollars on the table every year, overpaying for the health care of Church employees. The University of Notre Dame's Task Force (2006) report, *Making God Known, Loved, and Served,* echoed a similar theme.

The American bishops see the potential for seriously decreasing expenses in the area of health care, citing the Michigan Catholic Conference's work in this area (USCCB, 2005). The question has been approached before, but no serious attempts have succeeded beyond the Michigan dioceses (Nuzzi, 2008). The question is made even more salient by the fact that there is a network of Catholic hospitals in the United States, owned and operated by various church-affiliated groups, that has little leverage in determining the standard of care and costs for most diocesan health care plans. Even small steps in this area would help ameliorate the financial condition of most parishes with schools.

Similar economies of scale ought to be investigated and operationalized in other areas such as procurement of technology, purchasing of educational supplies, and the management of utility costs for electricity, natural gas, and water. The Mid-West Atlantic Consortium, a group of six east coast dioceses, has already demonstrated the benefits of forming an energy cooperative for the purposes of keeping utility costs low (www.midatlanticcsc.org/news_events/MACSC_news.html#energy).

Clearly, partnering in a regional or national cooperative for health care or natural gas procurement is not something every individual parish and pastor can accomplish. Leadership will be required at the diocesan, state, and national level. But since pastors have detailed knowledge about the fiscal struggles they are facing, they are in a position to push for reform in these areas where poor administration is resulting in expenses we can no longer sustain.

Increasing Revenues

Dioceses and individual schools are quickly coming of age in the areas of development and institutional advancement. These efforts are to be encouraged. Many schools, making due on tight budgets, often rely on the soft dollars of fundraising to provide the needed funds to balance the budget. Fundraising events, while meeting certain immediate needs, have their limits, and most successful institutions eventually adopt a more strategic approach to increasing revenue by creating a portfolio of development activities. These include capital campaigns, annual funds, giving societies, alumni associations, bequests and wills, grant writing, and foundation gifts. While efforts in Catholic school development are well underway, many struggling schools and parishes do not have the resources to begin on this path, even as they acknowledge its importance. Catholic philanthropy and Catholic colleges and universities can be helpful to parishes and schools in establishing these development services, especially in under-resourced communities. Pastors are particularly open to such meaningful partnerships with Catholic universities, which have recently not been very seriously engaged in many K-12 Catholic educational issues.

On a more national scale, increased revenues can be achieved through better accessing federal and state funds that are rightfully dedicated to providing services for students in Catholic schools. A variety of federal Title funds and numerous state funds across the nation are legally available for specified resources and services for Catholic school students. Often, because of the bureaucracy of the local public school system combined with the under-staffed offices of most dioceses and schools, Catholic school administrators lack the time and expertise to conduct the necessary investigation into accessing these funds. Moreover, because most Catholic schools span a variety of public school districts, applying for these funds can mean negotiating with several public school district administrators, despite legislation to the contrary. The financial result is that dollars that could be used for student services in Catholic schools are never acquired. Catholic school revenues could be increased, therefore, through a more concerted, strategic effort to access publicly available funds.

The politically sensitive issue of school choice is another ripe fruit, too long ignored by the Catholic sector. The Alliance for School Choice, a Washington, DC-based advocacy organization for school vouchers and tuition tax credit programs, reports that national momentum is well under way, working toward equality of educational opportunity for all students (www.allianceforschoolchoice. org). Since Catholic parents pay twice for their children's education—once through taxes and then again through tuition—some form of tax relief or tuition tax credits are highly desirable. Catholic educators and parents have many allies on this issue, including other families who support private schools. There are nearly 29,000 private schools in the United States, comprising 23% of all schools. These schools educate 6.2 million students, who represent approximately 11% of all students nationally (www.capenet.org). Strategic alliances across school sectors are needed to help establish equality of educational opportunity through a variety of school choice mechanisms such as vouchers and tax credits. While the official position of the Church has been to advocate for government support of schools as far back as Vatican Council II (1965), the Catholic community as a whole has not been energized and rallied in such a way as to make significant progress on this issue at the national level.

Similar to our recommendation on health care, political activity on behalf of school choice is not something that can be accomplished easily by a single parish or pastor. State legislatures have to be moved to action, the Catholic community mobilized, political leaders made to take notice, and all stakeholders persuaded to see the civic value in supporting religious schools with tax dollars. Some may argue that this recommendation is so challenging and fraught with such difficulties as to make any financial gains remote, if not impossible. We respond that the Catholic Church of Australia

U.S. Catholics, supported by their pastors and principals, and following the lead of their bishops, must embark on a similar mobilization in every state, to ensure the future of Catholic school education by working for school choice options that provide for just and equal educational opportunities for all students.

is currently celebrating 40 years of government funding for Catholic schools, in large part because of the nationwide radicalization of the Catholic population in the late 1960s on behalf of Catholic schools (Catholic Education Office, 2008). U.S. Catholics, supported by their pastors and principals, and following the lead of their bishops, must embark on a similar mobilization in every state, to ensure the future of Catholic school education by working for school choice options that provide for just and equal educational opportunities for all students.

One additional and novel possibility for increasing revenue is investments. As with health care plans, most dioceses manage their own investment funds in a pool that is limited to diocesan parishes and organizations. Recent recommendations emanating from business leaders and financial planners suggest that pooled investments may hold greater potential for growth (Notre Dame Task Force, 2006; www.nlrcm.org), something akin to a National Catholic Endowment Fund—a pooled vehicle for investing long-term assets of smaller Catholic colleges and universities, high schools, primary schools, and dioceses that can be managed using the "endowment model" popularized by the largest university endowment funds in the United States. Features of such a model include a wide array of diversification into both traditional and alternative investments such as stocks, bonds, private equity, hedge funds, real estate, commodities, emerging markets, etc. with access to top managers in each asset class. By pooling these assets and having strong oversight by experienced chief investment officers with access to the best in breed in each area, the funds have a much better risk/return profile due to size and oversight than they can achieve on their own. The assets would be managed in one pool which would be unitized like a mutual fund to provide the purchase and sale of units by each entity (Kochard & Rittereiser, 2008). Investment vehicles, terms, returns, administrative costs, and liquidity are all affected by the amount of capital available for investment by any one individual or juridic person. Dioceses, parishes, and schools may be more effective at increasing their annual return on investments by uniting to create larger endowments which could earn substantially higher returns because of the benefits that accrue to larger investment pools that are actively managed.

Recommendations in the Area of Faith and Catholic Identity

Because pastors are ultimately responsible for the pastoral care of everyone in the parish, their concerns about Catholic identity and faith formation must be taken seriously. Finances are undoubtedly burdensome for many, but we heard in strong language from hundreds of pastors just how important it was to them that Catholic schools serve as a leaven in the civic and ecclesial community. Pastors were pleased and supportive when school life and its attendant activities drew parents and families into full and active participation in Church life. They were less

> *Pastors were pleased and supportive when school life and its attendant activities drew parents and families into full and active participation in Church life.*

than enthusiastic and frequently irritated when the school became the sole locus for contact with the parish, even to the exclusion of Sunday Mass. Responding to the lived experience of pastors, our recommendations focus on adult and parental faith formation and education.

Conscious Integration of the School Community Into the Overall Life of the Parish

Catholic schools do not exist for themselves nor for their own self-perpetuation. They exist as ministries of the Church and participate in the overall evangelizing mission of the Church (Congregation for Catholic Education, 1997). It is imperative that Catholic schools be seen, experienced, and understood as deeply rooted in the life of a parish and as an integral part of the parish's larger pastoral services framework. Parish and school leaders can help advance this goal by establishing formal and informal lines of communication and cooperation that do not isolate parish ministries from each other. Even more proactively, budgets must reflect the goals of the parish and help incarnate its stated mission. Budgets are moral documents, educating the faithful regarding what is important to the community, and helping to prioritize the parish's approach to meeting competing demands for limited resources.

Broader Public Parish Leadership Roles for School Faculty, Staff, Administration, Students, and Parents

Those who work in, attend, and support Catholic schools cannot compartmentalize their commitment to the Church so that it is exclusively lived out in the context of the school alone. While school activities necessarily demand a high level of parental involvement and faculty supervision, school stakeholders must be encouraged and invited to assume more public and broader leadership roles in the life of the parish. In fact, one's commitment to the school ought to flow logically and freely from a larger commitment to the faith as it is experienced in parish life. The former cannot be a substitute for the latter. Such leadership and involvement by school stakeholders will also assist in the integration of the school into parish life in general.

Spiritual Renewal of Teachers and Administrators

Pastors were clear in their desire to operate Catholic schools, not private schools. Church teaching makes clear that a faculty plays an indispensable role in the Catholicity of the school, claiming that it is not what subjects that are taught in the building that make a school Catholic, but the people who work there (Congregation for Catholic Education, 1977). Regular sacramental celebrations and daily religion classes will add little to the Catholicity of a school if its faculty is not seen and experienced as living witnesses to Christ and the Church. Efforts at the parish, diocesan, regional, and national levels that sustain and strengthen the spiritual growth of the faculty and staff ought to be encouraged. This should involve ongoing education in the faith, prayer, and retreat opportunities, participation in the sacramental life of the Church, the parish leadership responsibilities described above, works of charity and justice, and an all encompassing vision, personally and professionally, that sees family life, world events, and common struggles as participation in the Paschal Mystery.

Education as a Model for All Ministry

In some important ways, every Church celebration and liturgical event is educational. Weddings teach about the love of God for the Church, reflected in the marital love of a couple. Funerals teach about the resurrection and Christ's victory over death, even as a loved one is laid to rest. Baptism teaches that the love of God embraces us well before we are ready to accept it of our own volition. Schools teach in more explicit ways and through many more subjects. Many parish ministries such as religious education, pre-marriage ministry, RCIA, youth ministry, and pastoral care have educational components that involve teaching of some sort. Education, then, may be understood as a model for all ministry. It is the Church's hope that all pastoral ministry is somehow educative and catechetical, that everything from sacramental celebrations to Church social groups plays some part in the ongoing faith formation and spiritual development of the parish community. Learning, about the faith, about oneself or one's community, ought not be limited to the school or to this year's class of adult converts. Ministry understood within this type of educational framework can help to better situate the school in the broader ministerial engagements of the parish, and help to focus the parish's contribution to the even broader evangelical mission of the Church.

Strategic Engagement of the Clergy in Support of Catholic Schools

If Catholic schools are to thrive and excel, and not simply survive, pastors, priests, and bishops must also be willing to engage the challenges facing schools in new and strategic ways. Leadership theory suggests that their role should involve the refinement and articulation of the mission, and of marshalling the resources needed to advance the mission.

An example of such leadership occurred during the timeframe of this study in the Diocese of Buffalo. After leading an extensive planning process, which resulted in the realignment and consolidation of many parishes and schools, Bishop Edward Kmiec reached out in a pastoral way to parents of the diocese, directly encouraging them to send their children to Catholic schools. In a letter dated July 28, 2008, and published in the diocesan newspaper *Western New York Catholic* he wrote to parents:

> Few choices in life are more important than deciding where to send your children to school. The education they receive has a lasting impact on their lives. If you haven't fully decided where your children will attend school this fall, **I strongly urge you to consider Catholic education.**
>
> I know that all parents want to give their children the benefit of an excellent education. But for Catholic parents, that's only the beginning. You also want your children to learn the values that will influence them for their entire life. That kind of faith-based education takes place every day in our Catholic schools. (p. 7, emphasis in original)

In recent years, such forthright and articulate advocacy for Catholic schools has not been common among diocesan bishops and parish pastors. In fact, a major recommendation from the University of Notre Dame's Task Force Report in 2006 focused exclusively on this same point. Under the heading "The Pastor, the Pulpit, and Parish Life," the Task Force wrote:

> We must find ways to promote Catholic schools without anxiety over offending those who may not share our passion. All pastors must be encouraged to endorse consistently and effectively the Bishop's position on Catholic schools. If our pastors and priests do not advocate for them in word and in deed, how can we expect more parishioners to enroll their children or increase their contributions to support the school?...The persistent support of pastors from the pulpit, the bulletin, and the parking lot is essential to enflame a renewed commitment among more lay men and women. (p. 15)

The leadership of the clergy remains an integral part of all Church activities and ministries, and Catholic schools cannot succeed without their vocal and consistent support. But what exactly should bishops and priests say and do, besides encouraging parents with school-age children to enroll their children in the local Catholic school? In an effort to synthesize the categories of finance and faith and answer this important question, we offer a closing analysis.

Finance and Faith as Expressions of a Deeper Challenge

In this study, we have attempted to summarize the views and concerns of U.S. pastors with oversight for Catholic schools. In doing so, we have learned much about the success of Catholic schools as well as the challenges that face them, and we have compared our findings across several areas with previous studies so that we might understand and uncover any new and salient dynamics that are at work in the parish leadership of the nation's pastors. Two major themes emerged in this study that best encapsulated the concerns of pastors: finances and faith. Pastors address the financial viability of schools every time they are engaged with tuition collection, enrollment management, fundraising, capital improvements, teacher salaries, and deferred maintenance, to name but a few major fiscal challenges.

These two themes of finances and faith are not unrelated. In fact, they may be understood as manifestations of a larger, singular issue that is impacting Catholic schools.

At the same time, pastors are highly committed to schools as instruments of evangelization and catechetical formation. They want to lead Catholic schools, not private schools. They desire that the schools be a leading vehicle in the parish for the engagement of families in the overall life of the parish community. They want the school to be an integral part of parish life and to serve as a leaven for the broader ecclesial and civic community.

These two themes of finances and faith are not unrelated. In fact, they may be understood as manifestations of a larger, singular issue that is impacting Catholic schools. Pastors experience it as the absence of school families from Sunday Mass. School parents experience it as the lack of strident support from the pastor. Parents and pastors alike articulate it when they complain about the ineffectiveness of the diocesan central office or the bishop. There is a widespread disengagement of Catholics from the Church and an equally challenging lack of appreciation for the wisdom, traditions, and teachings of the Catholic faith. This serious challenge is manifested in Catholic schools, but it is not limited to them. It can be seen in other arenas of Church life, such as religious vocations, marriage and divorce rates, social teachings, reproductive and sexual ethics, and in Church political engagements. In general, there appears to be a lack of serious adult engagement with the core beliefs of Catholicism that leads to a decline in the value of and participation in the life and ministry of the Church.

For example, Catholic theology affirms that at a certain point in history, God acted in an extraordinary way by becoming incarnate in the person of Jesus Christ. The Incarnation is, therefore, the focal point of human history. And it was not just a one time, historical event without consequences.

Catholics, and indeed all Christians, maintain that because of Jesus' Incarnation, all of life and all of history are somehow caught up in God's plan. There is an ongoing incarnation in our lives, an abiding presence of Jesus Christ, that challenges us to be attentive to the ongoing revelation of God in our lives. The Incarnation is a theological reality with imminently practical application.

The Gospels testify to the central events in Jesus' earthly life, his passion, death, and resurrection. Again, the Easter event, while clearly the focus of the New Testament, is not simply some biographical detail of long ago. It is a core conviction of faith and a central doctrine of Christianity that makes a difference in the life of believers today. Because of Jesus' resurrection, Christians believe in life after death, that suffering has meaning and purpose, and that this life is a participation in the dying and rising of Jesus. This conviction sustains the faithful, who see in their own life struggles a small but meaningful engagement with the Paschal Mystery.

From the point of view of the Incarnation and Paschal Mystery, Catholic schools and parishes strive to articulate and celebrate this deeper Christian anthropology that is a definitive worldview. If one fully understands the ramifications of the Incarnation and lives in the Paschal Mystery, seeing all the joys and sorrows of life as part and parcel of Jesus' death and resurrection, then Catholic parish life and Catholic school education make sense. They help, the Church says, to teach the truth, this truth: that Jesus Christ is at the center of our lives and is the sole reason these institutions exist. The choice is not between a parish and no parish, or between a Catholic school and a public school; the choice is between a deep immersion in the Paschal Mystery and an incarnational view of the world, or not. As regards a Catholic school education, this Christian anthropology touches every aspect of school life, so that not an hour goes by where the centrality of Jesus Christ to the Church and to each Christian is not indicated, honored, and celebrated.

A Catholic school is a Christian community, rooted in the person of Jesus Christ, established by the Church he founded, to educate and form the next generation about the central mysteries of life and faith.

The Catholic school is not a public school plus a religion curriculum and sacraments. It is not a private school with sectarian aims achieved by indoctrination. A Catholic school is a Christian community, rooted in the person of Jesus Christ, established by the Church He founded, to educate and form the next generation about the central mysteries of life and faith. A public school education, absent such a focus, is at best an incomplete education. At worst, it is an erroneous education for it excludes by constitutional mandate essential faith convictions about God and God's presence and action in history in Jesus Christ. And what can be predicated about the Catholic school is equally true of the Catholic parish. There is and ought to be a Christocentricity to Catholic life that no public institution can ever hope to claim.

For these reasons, we believe the more fundamental challenge facing Catholic schools in particular and the Church in general is theological. There is a manifest need for a greater appreciation and understanding of the central mysteries of the faith. There is a great need for adult education and conversion. There is an opportunity here for the renewal and re-engagement of adult Catholics with the faith, with schools, and with parishes. People routinely pay for what they value, be it a new flat screen television, a Catholic school education, or a European vacation. A new evangelization is needed, led by the clergy but engaging all, that emphasizes the core convictions of Catholicism, reclaims the basics truths of the faith, and develops a Catholic worldview in a way that modern families can understand and embrace. Understood this way, the most important leadership service the clergy can provide at this moment in our history is the evangelization and education of adult and young adult Catholics. A Catholicism fully understood, a Christianity fully realized, will lead adults, we believe, to a more robust participation in parish life, including enrollment of their children in Catholic schools. Clearly more research is needed to determine the most effective strategies and vehicles to deploy in the advancement of this opportunity in evangelization. Catholic colleges and universities, the philanthropic community, and leaders and stakeholders in Catholic institutions all have a role to play in the days ahead.

This is not to minimalize the financial concerns expressed by a significant number of pastors. Rather, it is to place the concern in context and help explain its power. The fiscal challenges facing so many parishes and schools are dramatic empirical indicators of the depth of this theological question. Schools are businesses, selling a product to customers. The balance sheet is a clear and quantifiable indicator of the value of the product being offered. This study leads us to hypothesize that it is the value proposition of Catholic education that has been lost, and that value proposition is highly theological in nature. By calling for the education and evangelization of adult and young adult Catholics, we hope to provide the inspiration for the renewal of both Catholic parishes and schools.

Closing Comments

We are grateful for the cooperation and support of so many of our colleagues in Catholic K-12 education and Catholic higher education. National studies are complicated undertakings, involving many stakeholders and touching on sensitive matters. We appreciate the collegial responses from dozens of dioceses and archdioceses, usually in the office of a superintendent or vicar, who generously assisted us in negotiating access to pastors. Principals, too, were often helpful and persistent colleagues in getting our survey into the hands of their pastors. For this invaluable assistance, we offer our heartfelt thanks.

Catholic schools remain the single most effective means of evangelization the Church has ever created. It seems only right that they provide the inspiration and rationale for the new evangelization called for today. In responding to the demands of finances and faith, we look forward to that day when, energized by a compelling and attractive incarnational faith, Catholic families live out their baptismal call by full and active participation in Catholic schools and Catholic parishes. We see this study then, not as advocacy for schools or for parishes, but as a call to reclaim, celebrate, and extol the truth and beauty of the Catholic faith. For these truths and for these deep mysteries, we readily advocate, for as loyal sons of the Church, sustained by decades of Catholic education, we can do no less.

References

Brausch, A. R. (2003, Winter). Parish administration: Theological foundations. *Church*, 24-27.

Buetow, H. A. (1970). *Of singular benefit: The story of Catholic education in the United States.* New York: Macmillan.

Buetow, H. A. (1985). *A history of United States Catholic schooling.* Washington, DC: National Catholic Educational Association.

Buetow, H. A. (1998). *The Catholic school: Its roots, identity, and future.* New York: Crossroad.

Caparros, E., Theriault, M., & Thorn, J. (Eds.). (1993). *The code of canon law.* Montreal, QC, Canada: Wilson & Lafleur.

Caruso, M. P. (2004a). Diocese and archdiocese. In T. Hunt, E. Joseph, & R. Nuzzi (Eds.), *Catholic schools in the United States: An encyclopedia* (pp. 227-229). Westport, CT: Greenwood.

Caruso, M. P. (2004b). Future shepherds and Catholic elementary schools. *Seminary Journal, 10*(1), 68-73.

Catholic Education Office, Sydney. (2008). *Celebrating 40 years of government financial assistance to Catholic schools in Sydney 1968-2008 and the role of Br. Kelvin Canavan in the continuing campaign.* Sydney, NSW, Australia: Author.

Christopher, L. (1997, October 17). Three deaneries begin second phase in Ministry 2000. *The Catholic Telegraph*, p. 7A.

Congregation for Catholic Education. (1977). *The Catholic school.* Washington, DC: United States Catholic Conference.

Congregation for Catholic Education. (1997). *The Catholic school on the threshold of the third millennium.* Rome: Libreria Editrice Vaticana.

Convey, J. J. (1999). Factors affecting the views of bishops and priests about Catholic schools. *Catholic Education: A Journal of Inquiry and Practice, 2*(3), 248-264.

DeLuca, B. (2001). Catholic school finance: A review of research. In T. Hunt, E. Joseph, & R. Nuzzi (Eds.), *Handbook of research on Catholic education* (pp. 229-262). Westport, CT: Greenwood.

Dillman, D. A. (2007). *Mail and Internet surveys: The tailored design method* (2nd ed.). Hoboken, NJ: John Wiley & Sons.

Gautier, M. (Ed.). (2008). College and graduate-level seminary students up slightly. *The CARA Report, 13*(4), 6.

Gray, M. M., & Gautier, M. L. (2006). *Primary trends, challenges and outlook: A report on Catholic elementary schools 2000-2005.* Washington, DC: Center for Applied Research in the Apostolate, Georgetown University.

Greeley, A. W., McCready, W. C., & McCourt, K. (1976). *Catholic schools in a declining church.* Kansas City, MO: Sheed & Ward.

Green, J. C., & Caracelli, V. J. (Eds.). (1997). *Advances in mixed-method evaluations: The challenges and benefits of integrating diverse paradigms.* San Francisco: Jossey-Bass.

Healey, T. J. (2008, September 8). A church transparent: What Catholic leaders have learned from the world of business. *America*, 26-27.

John Paul II. (1998). *Dies domini* [On keeping the Lord's day holy]. Boston: Pauline Books and Media.

Kmiec, E. (2008, August). Bishop Kmiec shares letter on Catholic education. *Western New York Catholic*, p. 7.

Kochard, L. E., & Rittereiser, C. (2008). *Foundation and endowment investing: Philosophies and strategies of top investors and institutions.* Hoboken, NJ: John Wiley & Sons.

Mallet, J. K.(1985, April). *Reflections on the application of the new code of canon law to the governance of Catholic educational institutions.* Address presented at the annual National Catholic Educational Association Convention, St. Louis, MO.

Mangione, T. W. (1998). Mail surveys. In L. Bickman & D. J. Rog (Eds.), *Handbook of applied social research methods* (pp. 399-427). Thousand Oaks, CA: Sage.

McDonald, D., & Schultz, M. M. (2008). *The annual statistical report on schools, enrollment, and staffing: United States Catholic elementary and secondary schools 2007-2008.* Washington, DC: National Catholic Educational Association.

McMahon, J. T. (1947). The priest visits his school. *The Catholic Educational Review, 45,* 451-457.

Miles, M. B., & Huberman, M. A. (1994). *Qualitative data analysis: An expanded sourcebook.* Thousand Oaks, CA: Sage.

National Conference of Catholic Bishops. (1972). *To teach as Jesus did: A pastoral message on Catholic education.* Washington, DC: United States Catholic Conference.

Notre Dame Task Force on Catholic Education. (2006). *Making God known, loved, and served: The future of Catholic primary and secondary schools in the United States.* Notre Dame, IN: University of Notre Dame.

Nuzzi, R. J. (2008). Responses from the field. *Catholic Education: A Journal of Inquiry and Practice, 11*(3), 325-332.

O'Brien, J. S. (1986). A study of the perceptions of bishops, pastors, and future pastors toward Catholic schools. (Doctoral dissertation, Virginia and Polytechnic Institute and State University). *Dissertation Abstracts International, 47,* 3928.

O'Brien, J. S. (1987). *Mixed messages: What bishops & priests say about Catholic schools.* Washington, DC: National Catholic Educational Association.

O'Brien, T. B. (1935). The pastor considers the parish school. *The Catholic Educational Review, 33,* 416-423.

Schipper, C. A. (1982). A study of the perception of Catholic schools by diocesan priests of the Archdiocese of San Francisco. (Doctoral dissertation, University of San Francisco). *Dissertation Abstracts International, 43,* 312.

Schonlau, M., Fricker, R. D., & Elliot, M. N. (2002). *Conducting research surveys via e-mail and the web.* Santa Monica, CA: RAND.

Study on parish-school governance executive summary. (2007). Unpublished manuscript, University of Notre Dame, Alliance for Catholic Education.

Sullivan, E. P. (1982). A study of the perceptions of Catholic schools by diocesan priests of the Archdiocese of Boston. (Doctoral dissertation, Boston College, 1981). *Dissertation Abstracts International, 42,* 3834.

Sweetser, T. P. (2007). *Keeping the covenant: Taking parish to the next level.* New York: Crossroad.

Sweetser, T. P., & Holden, C. M. (1992). *Leadership in a successful parish* (2nd ed.). Franklin, WI: Sheed and Ward.

Sweetser, T. P., & McKinney, M. B. (1998). *Changing pastors: A resource for pastoral transitions.* Franklin, WI: Sheed and Ward.

Tacheny, T. S. (1987). A study of the perceptions of Catholic schools by diocesan priests of the Winona and New Ulm dioceses of Minnesota (Doctoral dissertation, Saint Louis University, 1987). *Dissertation Abstracts International, 48,* 802.

United States Conference of Catholic Bishops. (2005). *Renewing our commitment to Catholic elementary and secondary schools in the third millennium.* Washington, DC: Author.

Unrau, Y. A., & Coleman, H. (1997). Qualitative data analysis. In R. M. Grinell, Jr. (Ed.), *Social work research and evaluation: Quantitative and qualitative approaches* (5th ed., pp. 501-526). Itasca, IL: Peacock.

Vatican Council II. (1965). *Gravissimum educationis* [Declaration on Christian education]. Boston: St. Paul.

Walch, T. (1996). *Parish school: American Catholic parochial education from colonial times to the present.* New York: Crossroad.

Zech, C., & Miller, R. (2007, Summer). The professional development needs of pastors and business managers. *Church,* CS1-CS6.

Appendix A

Survey Instrument

University of Notre Dame Study of U.S. Pastors

Section 1: Introduction

You are invited to participate in a study of pastors of schools conducted by the Institute for Educational Initiatives at the University of Notre Dame. You have been selected for participation because the Arch(Bishop) and/or Superintendent of your diocese provided contact information for pastors with oversight for schools.

The purpose of this study is to explore and understand the needs, perceptions, and attitudes of pastors with oversight for Catholic schools. According to the Code of Canon Law, the pastor is responsible for education in his parish. A clear and nuanced understanding of their needs, challenges, and leadership insights is required.

If you decide to participate, this survey should take approximately 15 minutes to complete. There are no risks associated with participation in the study. Survey questions ask for reflections on attitudes, perceptions, and reflections on personal opinions. There are no items of a sensitive nature. Although individual participants may feel gratified with sharing their opinions and insights, there is no immediate benefit to participants. The larger benefit of the study is increased knowledge of the dynamics facing pastors with Catholic schools so that the University of Notre Dame is better informed to serve and meet those needs.

You are free to refuse to participate or to withdraw your consent to participate in this research at any time without penalty or prejudice; your participation is entirely voluntary. Information that is obtained from you in connection with this study will remain confidential. Your privacy will be protected because you will not be identified by name as a participant in this project. Data from the survey will be reported only in aggregate form and your responses will not be identified individually.

If you have any questions, you may contact Rev. Ronald Nuzzi at 574-631-7730 or pastors@nd.edu.

Having read the information provided above, please provide your consent to participate by clicking "Next."

Section 2: General Background Information

Questions 1-20 are designed to provide relevant background information for the overall study.

1. What is your age?

2. What is the zip code for your current parish?

3. How many years have you been ordained a priest?

4. Are you a diocesan or religious priest?

◯ Diocesan

◯ Religious

5. Where did you attend seminary?

City, State

City, State

University of Notre Dame Study of U.S. Pastors

6. Did you attend a Catholic elementary school?

◯ Did not attend

◯ 1-2 years

◯ 3-4 years

◯ 5-6 years

◯ 7-8 years

7. Did you attend a Catholic high school?

◯ Did not attend

◯ 1-2 years

◯ 3-4 years

8. Did you attend a Catholic college or university before seminary?

◯ Did not attend

◯ 1-2 years

◯ 3-4 years

◯ 5 years or more

9. Have you ever taught in a Catholic school?

◯ Yes   ◯ No

Number of years

[   ]

10. Have you ever been an administrator of a Catholic school?

◯ Yes   ◯ No

Number of years

[   ]

11. Have you ever been a chaplain or campus minister for a Catholic school?

◯ Yes   ◯ No

Number of Years

[   ]

12. Have you ever been superintendent of Catholic schools?

◯ Yes   ◯ No

Number of years

[   ]

University of Notre Dame Study of U.S. Pastors

13. Have you ever worked in the diocesan office or chancery?

◯ Yes   ◯ No

Number of Years

[   ]

14. How many years have you served in a parish with a school?

[   ]

15. How many years have you been pastor at your current parish?

[   ]

16. How many students are currently enrolled at your school?

[   ]

17. Approximately what percentage of the student population in your school is Roman Catholic?

[   ]

18. What is the primary race/ethnicity of the student population at your current school?

◯ American Indian

◯ Hispanic or Latino

◯ Asian or Asian American

◯ Caucasian

◯ Black or African American

◯ Other

Please specify

[   ]

19. How is your current school structured?

◯ Pre-K to 6th

◯ Pre-K to 8th

◯ K to 6th

◯ K to 8th

Other (please specify)

[   ]

University of Notre Dame Study of U.S. Pastors

20. Which best describes the location of your current school?

◯ Inner city: Area located within the central portion of a major city generally characterized by a large proportion of low income inhabitants

◯ Urban, but not inner city: Located within the limits of a major city, but not in an area characterized as inner-city

◯ Suburban: Located outside the city limits of a major city

◯ Small town or rural: Located in an area that is not considered a suburb

Section 3: Needs Assessment

Questions 21-28 are designed to provide relevant information regarding the major areas of need at your current school.

21. Rate the importance of each need area as it pertains to your parish school

	Extremely important	Very important	Moderately important	Somewhat important	Not at all important
Governance	◯	◯	◯	◯	◯
Catholic identity	◯	◯	◯	◯	◯
Long-range planning	◯	◯	◯	◯	◯
Marketing	◯	◯	◯	◯	◯
Capital improvements	◯	◯	◯	◯	◯
Enrollment management	◯	◯	◯	◯	◯
Financial management	◯	◯	◯	◯	◯
Faculty recruitment and retention	◯	◯	◯	◯	◯
Development	◯	◯	◯	◯	◯
Technology	◯	◯	◯	◯	◯
Board management	◯	◯	◯	◯	◯
Parental involvement	◯	◯	◯	◯	◯
Assessment	◯	◯	◯	◯	◯
Inclusion/special needs students	◯	◯	◯	◯	◯
Alumni organization	◯	◯	◯	◯	◯
Professional development for faculty	◯	◯	◯	◯	◯

22. From the checklist below indicate the top five (5) areas that your parish school is currently addressing:

☐ Governance ☐ Financial management ☐ Assessment

☐ Catholic identity ☐ Faculty recruitment and retention ☐ Inclusion/special needs students

☐ Long-range planning ☐ Development ☐ Alumni organization

☐ Marketing ☐ Technology ☐ Professional development for faculty

☐ Capital improvements ☐ Board management

☐ Enrollment management ☐ Parental involvement

University of Notre Dame Study of U.S. Pastors

23. In your own words, what are the most important NEEDS facing your parish school in the next two to five years?

24. Does your school currently have any relationship with an institution of higher education (college or university)?

◯ Yes   ◯ No

Which college or university?

25. Do you perceive the mission of your school to be supported by Catholic institutions of higher education (colleges and /or universities)?

◯ Yes   ◯ No

In what regard?

26. What kind of assistance would you accept from Catholic colleges and universities regarding your needs? Check all that apply.

☐ Diocesan conference/workshop

☐ Regional conference/workshop

☐ Written materials

☐ University-based conference/workshop

☐ Web-based resources

☐ Consulting services

Other:

27. What is your most reliable source of information for decision making regarding your school?

◯ Bishop   ◯ Parent/teacher organization

◯ Central office   ◯ Other pastors and priests

◯ Principal   ◯ University contacts

◯ Superintendent   ◯ Professional organizations

◯ School board

Other:

University of Notre Dame Study of U.S. Pastors

28. In regard to school matters, rate the level of support and backing that you receive from each of the following:

	Highest support	Moderate support	Minimal support	No support
Bishop	○	○	○	○
Superintendent	○	○	○	○
Principal	○	○	○	○
Central office	○	○	○	○
Other pastors and priests	○	○	○	○
Parents	○	○	○	○
Parish council	○	○	○	○
School board	○	○	○	○

Section 4: Perceptions and Attitudes

Directions: Questions 29-33 are designed to provide relevant information regarding perceptions of and attitudes toward Catholic schools and education.

29. Please rate the following statements regarding Catholic schools

	Strongly agree	Agree	Neutral	Disagree	Strongly Disagree
The need for Catholic schools is at least as great today as in the past.	○	○	○	○	○
Catholic schools are worth what it costs to operate them.	○	○	○	○	○
Maintaining Catholic schools is an effective use of diocesan and parish resources.	○	○	○	○	○
Catholic schools are an essential part of the Church's educational ministry.	○	○	○	○	○
In addition to the family, Catholic schools are the best means for the religious formation of the young.	○	○	○	○	○
The Catholic school is one of the best means of evangelization in the Church today.	○	○	○	○	○
I enjoy being the pastor of a parish that has a Catholic school.	○	○	○	○	○

University of Notre Dame Study of U.S. Pastors

30. Please rate the following statements regarding Catholic schools

	Strongly agree	Agree	Neutral	Disagree	Strongly Disagree
Most Catholic schools that I know seem to teach Catholic doctrine reasonably well.	○	○	○	○	○
The Catholic schools that I know have effective programs of religious formation.	○	○	○	○	○
Most Catholic schools that I know seem to have well-prepared and effective teachers.	○	○	○	○	○
Most Catholic schools that I know seem to have a strong Catholic identity.	○	○	○	○	○
Most Catholic schools that I know seem to have well-prepared and effective principals.	○	○	○	○	○
Most Catholic schools that I know seem to have clear goals and priorities.	○	○	○	○	○

31. Please rate the following statements regarding Catholic schools

	Strongly agree	Agree	Neutral	Disagree	Strongly Disagree
Every parish should provide some financial support for Catholic schools.	○	○	○	○	○
In areas where there is only one Catholic school and several parishes, each of the parishes should financially support the school.	○	○	○	○	○
The financial support of Catholic schools is the duty of all Catholics whether or not they have children in the schools.	○	○	○	○	○
Some of the surplus of affluent parishes should be shared with financially struggling parishes that support Catholic schools.	○	○	○	○	○
A parish without a Catholic school should financially assist Catholic schools that enroll its students.	○	○	○	○	○
The maintenance of Catholic schools in poor, inner-city areas should be a diocesan priority.	○	○	○	○	○

University of Notre Dame Study of U.S. Pastors

32. Please rate the following statements regarding Catholic schools

	Strongly agree	Agree	Neutral	Disagree	Strongly Disagree
Parents should have a substantial voice in the governance of Catholic schools.	◯	◯	◯	◯	◯
Parents must be given a substantial role in the development of policy for Catholic schools.	◯	◯	◯	◯	◯
All Catholic schools should have school boards/councils.	◯	◯	◯	◯	◯
When a school serves several parishes, a representative board/council should be responsible for the school's governance.	◯	◯	◯	◯	◯

33. Please provide any additional comments regarding thoughts and opinions on Catholic schools and Catholic school leadership.

Appendix B

Additional Open-Ended Question Sub-Themes (6 through 10)

General Governance

Pastors commented on general governance in 43 text segments. The subject seemed to be one that pastors generally did not have common ideas about. The discussion revolved around many issues regarding what constitutes good governance and who is responsible for stability of governance. Responses varied greatly and pastors expressed widely differing views on this subject. However, most pastors that commented on the subject agreed that there is a crisis in governance in Catholic schools. Although many made suggestions for new models of governance, those also varied greatly.

In response to the question of who is responsible for providing good governance in Catholic schools, pastors offered several different answers. Some felt that school boards are responsible, others felt that the pastor/principal is responsible, others still felt that the diocese is responsible, and some felt that a combination of the three is responsible. Those who commented on the responsibility of school boards generally agreed that boards as they exist today are flawed. One pastor said, "I think that in all schools, public, Catholic and private, school boards are a negative factor, leading to incompetent micro-management by unqualified, inexperienced and often personally motivated individuals." Many pastors agreed that the power of school boards should be limited, as they "need to be much better trained in their specific roles and responsibility." Some pastors felt that school boards are still useful, but only in particular and very specific functions. One pastor cited the role of a school board as "policy making," and another said, "a board that is representative of the school population can be very helpful in developing policy." Several responses mentioning school boards used the adjective "advisory" to describe the role of school boards. One pastor commented that "our school board is called an advisory committee," and another said,

> Schools should have boards that function as advisory to the principal. They should be responsible for obtaining funds and promotion. They should recommend the tuition to the pastor who alone sets it. The boards must be advisory and not micromanage; the role of the principal as reporting directly only to the pastor must be maintained.

Several pastors felt that the responsibility for good governance in Catholic schools fell to the pastor and/or principal solely. One pastor said, "Catholic schools must remain clearly and absolutely under

Note. Written with the assistance of Margaret A. Solic, Undergraduate Research Assistant, Institute for Educational Initiatives, University of Notre Dame.

the control of a local pastor or the local ordinary," while another commented, "The responsibility for governance falls to the pastor," while still another explained, "As long as accountability in the Church remains drawn as it is now, I think policy and governance must be heavily in the hands of the pastor and principal." However, for this model of governance to work, the relationship between the pastor and the principal must be a positive one. One pastor remarked, "Governance is a big issue. Catholic school principals are asked to do a great deal without a lot of support. If the pastor is not supportive, it leaves the administration high and dry." Another pastor added, "Constant communication is essential between pastor and principal. The pastor needs to let the principal do his/her job without micro-managing."

The term "micro-managing" showed up frequently in all of the responses regarding general governance. Pastors seemed to be fairly concerned about the interaction between pastors, principals, and school boards. Therefore, they also suggested new models of governance, most of which included the diocese taking part or full responsibility for stability of governance. One pastor cited differences between the principal and pastor of a school as the reason for suggesting diocesan control of governance. He said, "The worst case scenario is a parish where the pastor is actively working against the success of the school....As a result, I believe that all parochial schools in a diocese should be 'diocesan' and the direct responsibility of the Superintendent and the Office of Catholic Schools." The same pastor went on to outline a plan for how the diocese would govern Catholic schools. He explained,

> The parishes should be expected to continue to provide financial support, the priests, especially the pastors, should be expected to continue to provide a presence and sacramental guidance and support, but the operation of the system, from the hiring of principals and maintenance of buildings, to final decisions on expulsions should be handled through a central office, (i.e., the Catholic Schools Office), and not involve the office of the local pastor.

Several pastors agreed that governance should be administered by some sort of central office, and some described systems that already used this new model. However, there were some other suggestions for new models of governance. One pastor described a K-12 model spread over three campuses, led by a single president and three principals. Another commented, "The beginning of regional Catholic schools seems more advantageous to me. They would have their own Boards (perhaps with reps from the local parishes). They would also have their own Finance Council and Board and be financially responsible for their existence." Although these few models combine boards, pastors, principals, and the diocese, most of the recommended new models emphasized the role of the diocese in governing Catholic schools over any other role.

Parish-School-Parent Connections

Comments regarding the relationships among the parish, the parish school, and parents were mentioned in 42 text segments. Pastors largely commented on the lack of school parents' connection to and involvement with the broader parish. While some spoke of the lack of faith education at home, others cited a general lack of parish support, while still others expressed frustration with the lack of attendance at Sunday Mass by school-going children and their families (as discussed in a previous theme). Pastors also frequently mentioned the need for a more cohesive linkage between the parish school and the parish as a whole, highlighting in particular the need to be of one accord financially.

Fully aligned with the earlier theme—School Families Need to Attend Sunday Mass—many pastors defined participation in the parish solely as going to Mass on Sunday. One pastor said, "I judge Catholicity by Sunday Mass attendance," while another commented, "[Parents] do not actively practice their faith, that is, rarely do I see some of these parents at Sunday Mass." Pastors emphasized that this lack of parental support in faith education, Mass attendance, and other parish activities stemmed from their displacement of values in choosing a Catholic education for their children. Many acknowledged that parents choose Catholic schools for their children because they can serve as a "stepping stone to an influential high school and college." Pastors also felt as if parents were using Catholic schools to avoid sending their children to public schools. Catholic schools, some pastors felt, provide a "safer environment" and are seen as "private schooling at reduced cost." Whatever the reason parents chose Catholic education for their children, pastors felt as if the most important one had been forgotten: "Many parishioners really miss the point of a Catholic parish grade school," one said. "That point being the ability and opportunity to teach and mold the future generations in the way of Jesus."

Aligned with their perception that parents do not seem to understand the true purpose of a Catholic education, pastors also felt that parents were not committed to providing faith education at home. Many pastors seemed to feel as if parents thought that sending their children to Catholic school was sufficient to instill good values. One pastor explained, "Parents must better embrace their role as primary faith formation and better involve their families in the life of the parish. It seems that since they send their children to Catholic schools, their responsibility ends with tuition payments." Most pastors felt that schools could be an excellent evangelization tool if only parents would participate equally. One pastor articulated this point well when he said, "Parents too often have the attitude of being a consumer of Catholic education rather than embracing responsibility for its continuance and development."

Disappointment in and frustration with parents for not stressing evangelization permeated the responses. Since the point of Catholic education is to provide a quality education while forming conscious, moral, and strongly faithful Catholic citizens, some pastors wondered if the effort was worth the cost. "In essence, the effort of Catholic education is often in vain because the Catholic values and faith knowledge taught...in school are not reinforced at home." The same pastor went on to say,

> Rather than adding vibrance to the faith community they end up sucking the life out of the parish. I, and I think many others, would strongly support Catholic schools if they were a more efficient and effective means of instilling strong Catholic identity, faith formation and parish involvement that encompassed the whole family. Sadly, many Catholic schools don't or can't meet those basic standards because of the lack of leadership or parental support.

The absence of parental involvement in many aspects of the parish-school-parent connection seemed to be the primary impediment for pastors to providing a true Catholic education for their students.

Pastors also felt as if there was a lack of connection between parishes and schools. Several pastors commented that "there seemed to be a strong disconnect between a school life and parish life." Pastors believed that a connection between the school and the parish was as important to the success of that school as the connection between parents and the parish. One pastor went so far as to say, "The future of the Church is in Catholic education….I believe that no other program can secure the future of Catholic parishes." Parishes provide some financial support for the schools; however, most pastors felt that was where the connection ended. One even complained, "As far as I am concerned the parishes I have dealt with treat the school as a community unto itself with no desire to work with the parish or the pastor UNTIL they get into trouble." Pastors felt that schools needed to allow the parish to support them in ways other than just financially. "We [pastors] have to know what we are doing and be willing to support. At the same time, the school must remain an integral part of the parish and not try to stand by itself."

Consolidation and Regionalization

In 41 text segments, pastors expressed widely divergent views regarding the consolidation and regionalization of parish schools. Pastors' statements were easily classified into positive, negative, and neutral reactions. Twenty-six of the pastors felt positively about consolidation and regionalization, 11 of the pastors felt negatively, and 4 of the pastors expressed neutral opinions. Speaking from their experiences either in or among consolidated schools, pastors firmly expressed their opinions about this issue.

Pastors generally saw consolidated/regional schools as one of the best solutions to ensure the future of Catholic education. As one pastor noted, "My parish is part of a multi-parish school. I believe this is the best option for the future of elementary Catholic education….The traditional parochial school model needs to be re-thought to remain vital, competitive, and balanced." Another pastor spoke of the need to strengthen Catholic schools and give them the proper tools to succeed by pooling resources and consolidating. He says,

> A parish school is the life-blood of the parish, and it is essential that it is supported….The diocese must work to strengthen Catholic schools, even if it means closing some smaller schools and combining them with other schools in order to strengthen the overall health of the Catholic school system.

Another pastor repeated the same sentiment when he acknowledged that Catholic schools are "in competition with each other rather than working together for the good of the community in a given area." He outlined a plan for schools to be structured by the diocese, where each school would follow a set tuition policy and payment plan and that gives the diocese primary responsibility for finances and governance in order to strengthen and standardize the entire system. The opinion that the Catholic education system has become outdated was reinforced when another pastor said,

> The heyday of Catholic elementary and secondary schools disappeared when the cheap labor of sisters and brothers had to be replaced by full-salaried lay employees….Catholic schools are important, but in many places the structural model of the schools must undergo change.

Several negative statements cited lack of Catholic, parish, or school identity as being problematic in consolidated/regional schools. One pastor stated,

> The Catholic school in a parish serves as a focus for community in the parish….In a parish with a school it means that the parish community is strengthened by the presence of the school and its students have a stronger Catholic identity since they participate in the spiritual life of the parish.

While pastors acknowledged the financial difficulties of running parish schools, they also felt strongly that Catholic schools should be an integral part of the parish's mission. One pastor stated, "I believe that Catholic schools should be parochial schools—they are an extension of the catechetical ministry of the pastor and the parish." These pastors feared a loss of Catholic identity and a dilution of parish affiliation that may emerge in consolidated/regional schools.

Financial viability of parish schools was noted as the main reason pastors were supportive of consolidated schools. Almost half of the 41 responses mentioned financial concerns as a motive for supporting consolidated or regional schools. As one pastor summarized,

> The Catholic school as we know it is doomed for the land of dinosaurs unless we develop new strategies for regional Catholic schools, supplemented by several parishes and open to such. It won't be long before individual parishes will not be able to subsidize, nor will parents be able to afford, the costs of a Catholic school in their midst.

Pastors were overwhelmingly concerned with two things: surviving financially on parish funds and donations, and ensuring that Catholic schools would be financially available to all students of all income levels. One pastor suggested that "putting responsibility for its [regional school's] finances in the hands of the diocese would be more equitable and would demonstrate the Church's desire not just to maintain Catholic education, but to foster its availability for all Catholics and others as well." Another pastor suggested "the other alternative is to charge the full cost for each student" but also acknowledged that the consequence of that would be that "our schools become very elitist." He pointed out, "If we are going to offer parish support, we should be striving to keep it possible for the average family." And yet another pastor noted, "The support of all parishes will be important if Catholic education is to be accessible for Catholics of all income levels."

However supportive the pastors were about consolidated schools, they noted several additional challenges that emerge with these new models. In particular, pastors expressed concerns regarding the governance of the school. Some pastors mentioned models that worked efficiently and some pastors mentioned models that did not work efficiently. One pastor said, "We are reluctant to give parents substantive participation in school governance. One of the pastors dominates and 'runs things' with the principal." However, another described, "We have recently adopted a K-12 model of one school with three campuses. We have a single president and three principals. It is an effective means of governance that has led to school growth and better programs." Another pastor explained the difficulties with school governance. "There is a Governing Board comprised of the two pastors, parish administrators and a Finance Council member from each parish. The Governing Board functions as the pastor would in a single parish school. However, it is difficult to run a school by committee."

Alternative Ways to Evangelize

In 33 text segments, pastors spoke about the need to find alternative ways to evangelize. Pastors' concern about rethinking evangelization arose out of their doubts regarding the effectiveness of Catholic schools as well as the equity of distribution of funds in parishes. One pastor summed it up,

> In this day and age, with great public schools…I am hard pressed to understand the need of every parish trying to maintain a school. I have 1,400 children in Religious Education on Saturday morning. But I have limited resources to provide greater assistance to them because we spend so much on the school for 280 students.

Two pastors drew on the history of Catholic schools to argue for a reevaluation of the current system. They both claimed that the traditional Catholic school model is outdated because anti-Catholic and anti-immigrant sentiment no longer exists the way it did when Catholic schools were founded. One cited Catholic schools' 19th century ascent in the face of blatant anti-Catholicism, a context that has greatly changed today. The second pastor challenged others to question, "As immigrants we were denied a public school education as third class citizens. What effect did that have on our current model and philosophy? And have we reached a point to revisit that philosophy?"

Many of the pastors who commented on alternative ways to evangelize believe that the Catholic Church has reached an opportune point to revisit that philosophy. Most called for a refocusing of Catholic faith education and a reallocation of resources in order to more equally serve Catholic parishes. Language to describe the failings of the current system utilized phrases such as "justice," "effectiveness," "worth," "efficient," "neglect," and "equitable distribution of funds." Pastors felt that the current system neglected most of the parish, since a large amount of parish funds went toward the Catholic school that serves only a small percentage of the parish. One pastor explained, "There is also a question of justice. So many resources go to educate a few children in all subjects, and so few go to provide faith formation for all children, youth, and adults."

Almost all of the pastors suggested a move from the formal structure of Catholic schools to a more informal and, they thought, more effective way to evangelize. Several pastors expressed the idea that scant resources could be much more efficiently used if they were put toward religious education programs. Pastors acknowledged that "often our resources can be better served in other ways in evangelizing our communities," and that "Religious Education programs would be a far better use of parish and diocesan resources."

For these pastors, effective use of parish and diocesan resources means that funds would be taken away from Catholic schools and distributed more equally within the parish. From that, funds would be allocated for a "much ramped-up religious education program." Suggestions ranged from "I am hard pressed to understand the need of every parish trying to maintain a school," to "I wonder how much more effective our parish efforts would be if we could redirect some monies from the Catholic school to parish programs and staff that could do a more effective job of evangelization." Most pastor comments centered on the necessity of redirecting funds in some way, whether totally or partially, to religious education programs.

Pastors acknowledged that religious education programs, as they exist today, have the potential to reach more youth than Catholic schools; however, they also need to be rethought and restructured to achieve that goal. One pastor stated,

I strongly believe that the Catholic schools concept needs to refocus. Given the fact that a very low percentage of Catholic children receive education in Catholic schools and that the alternative, "Christian Formation (CCD)" is largely ineffective…there needs to be a new model for sharing our faith.

Many acknowledged the need to expand religious educations programs beyond one hour a week; however, few proposed solutions. One pastor did make a suggestion:

In Pennsylvania, there is a law on the books ("Release Time") that allows for students to be released from their public school and bused to a regional center for one hour of religious education.…The Archdiocese should establish regional religious centers throughout the Archdiocese with qualified, paid religious education teachers who would staff these centers 5 days a week on a full-time basis in order to accommodate the many public schools and varied time schedules of these schools.

Most pastors did not have such a detailed approach to the problem and simply wanted Catholics to rethink the current system in order to find a better way to use resources and evangelize.

Suggestions for new models of evangelization ranged from the redirection of parish funds to religious education programs to ideas about expanding evangelization beyond school-age children. One pastor noted, "There needs to be a new model for sharing our faith. We need to pool resources and sharpen our focus on families and adults that have been short-changed in Christian formation," while another suggested, "more emphasis should be placed on the fostering of family life by one-day family building mini-retreats involving parents and students." Some pastors simply expressed frustration with the current system, saying, "I am not totally convinced that one-hour per week religious education is effective," and "I am certainly open to other forms of faith formation, but if not schools, then what? Show me something that works."

Ensuring Access and Affordability

Comments about ensuring access and affordability in Catholic schools were mentioned in 32 text segments. Pastors were largely concerned about three things: that Catholic schools are primarily becoming schools for the rich and affluent, that Catholic schools need to remember their mission to serve low-income families, and that Catholic schools need to provide financial aid to ensure access and affordability.

Pastors commented extensively on the concern that, due to financial strains on low to middle class families, Catholic schools are becoming schools for the wealthy only. They were apprehensive of "leaning to the rich." One pastor remarked, "We seem to be closer to sponsoring 'elitist' schools simply because of the average parent being unable to keep digging deeper," while another pastor said, "Catholic education is becoming an education for the rich or elite while many of our middle class families struggle to keep their children in our Catholic school or drop out altogether." A few pastors were concerned that Catholic schools were leaving out a large population (i.e., middle class) by focusing on educating the poor as well as educating those who can afford to pay tuition. One pastor said, "Our current model will effectively lead us into Catholic education for the very poor, by our [religious communities'] commitment to the poor; and education for the rich." Another commented,

"These schools tend to provide service to those who can afford tuition and to the inner-city poor. A large part of the Catholic population may want the school but cannot afford it." However, most pastors' fears about the affordability of a Catholic education led them to worry if Catholic schools were fulfilling their mission of serving the poor. One pastor vehemently commented, "Some schools…are too costly to attend and though they may be Catholic they aren't catholic. They are only for the rich and leave the poor behind. I refuse to support a school only for the rich as being part of the Church's mission."

Out of this concern arose several comments regarding the Church's need to reemphasize its focus on Catholic education for the poor. One pastor stated, "We must find a way to make Catholic schools available for any family who desires them," while another pastor expressed, "It is difficult to keep the costs at a level where the majority of the people can attend a Catholic school." Most pastors cited a "responsibility to give the low income child an opportunity to have a Catholic education," and discussed this responsibility in regard to the moral mission of the Catholic Church. Some pastors talked about not only serving children from low-income families, but also acknowledged a wider social issue. One said, "The other area I want to address is making my school possible for the poor Mexicans and African Americans. They deserve the same opportunity as I did. It cannot be just for the well off." Another pastor noted,

> The failure of our schools…really makes me wonder why we dump so much resource into keeping them open to serve what is more and more a privileged elite. In this area, it seems our blue collar families have drifted away because the parishes were focused on keeping a school open that the blue collar families could never hope to enjoy, and because our teaching of doctrine was so weak that it appeared Catholicism had nothing left to offer them.

In response to this problem, several pastors suggested coming up with financial aid plans to ensure access and affordability for all who want a Catholic education. One pastor suggested that "parents who can afford to pay the 'true cost' of educating their children should come as close as possible to doing so, so that any support from parish(es) can be placed into a fund for scholarships." Pastors who commented on the need for financial aid generally felt that any parish or diocesan support should not go to the school itself, but rather to those families who cannot afford tuition. One pastor remarked, "I think that most of the parish support for Catholic school education should be in the form of tuition assistance to families in need, not direct aid to the schools." Another spoke of the need to restructure the way Catholic schools are financed to ensure access and affordability. He said,

> Schools that are a financial burden on a parish and that lack Catholic teachers and students… should probably be closed.…It doesn't seem to be good stewardship of parish resources to support such schools. We should, instead, support those schools that are successful and redirect diocesan resources in the form of financial aid to Catholic families.

The pastors who commented on the need for financial aid seemed to think that this redirection of parish resources would be an important step in ensuring access and affordability for all who wish to have a Catholic education, regardless of family income level.

About the Authors

Ronald J. Nuzzi is a priest of the Diocese of Youngstown, Ohio. He is Director of The Mary Ann Remick Leadership Program in the Alliance for Catholic Education at the University of Notre Dame. A nationally known speaker and scholar, Nuzzi has led dozens of staff development days, in-services, and retreats for Catholic school teachers and administrators in the United States, Canada, Mexico, and Italy. He holds a Ph.D. in Educational Administration from the University of Dayton and Master's degrees in Philosophy, Theology, and Education.

James M. Frabutt is Faculty in The Mary Ann Remick Leadership Program in the Alliance for Catholic Education and Concurrent Associate Professor of Psychology at the University of Notre Dame. He previously served as Deputy Director of the Center for Youth, Family, and Community Partnerships at the University of North Carolina at Greensboro. He has employed action-oriented, community-based research approaches to areas such as juvenile delinquency prevention, school-based mental health, teacher/administrator inquiry, racial disparities in the juvenile justice system, and community violence reduction. He holds a Master's degree and Ph.D. in Human Development and Family Studies from the University of North Carolina at Greensboro.

Anthony C. Holter is Faculty in The Mary Ann Remick Leadership Program in the Alliance for Catholic Education and Concurrent Assistant Professor of Psychology at the University of Notre Dame. A graduate of the Alliance for Catholic Education, Holter taught at Holy Trinity Catholic Middle School in Charlotte, North Carolina. He holds a Ph.D. in Educational Psychology from the University of Wisconsin-Madison and Master's degrees in Education and Educational Psychology.

Correspondence concerning *Faith, Finances, and the Future: The Notre Dame Study of U.S. Pastors* should be addressed to Rev. Ronald J. Nuzzi, Ph.D., University of Notre Dame, 154 Institute for Educational Initiatives Building, Notre Dame, IN 46556.

Printed in the United States
127537LV00002B/341-3700/P